TAIL-WAGGING GOOD TREAT RECIPES

Proud Dog Chef

By: Proud Dog Mom

Proud Dog Chef
Tail-Wagging Good Treat Recipes

Published in the United States of America by Proud Press Publishing,
a division of Proud Dog Mom, LLC in South Carolina.
www.ProudPressPublishing.com
www.ProudDogMom.com

First Edition

ISBNs:
978-0-9998409-0-0 (hardcover)
978-0-9998409-2-4 (paperback)
978-0-9998409-1-7 (eBook)

Design by Jera Publishing
Treat styling by Proud Dog Mom
Food photography by Proud Dog Mom
Lifestyle photography by Peaberry Photo

Disclaimer: The book's writers and creators are not liable for the use or misuse of the information in this book. Before introducing new ingredients to your dog's diet, always check with your local veterinarian. While this book is filled with recipes that are considered healthy for the average dog, every canine's nutritional needs are different.

Table of Contents

Becoming A Dog Chef

I remember as a little girl hearing the click-clacking sound of dog nails hitting against the hardwood floors of my family home. They followed me everywhere—to the bedroom late at night to sleep by my side; to the bathroom in the morning to keep me company; to the kitchen throughout the day in hopes of sharing my meals. *Seriously, how do people without dogs keep the floors clean?!* At that time, my family had a 150 pound Great Dane and a five pound Yorkshire Terrier. What a duo, right? Those two made life more exciting. They filled our house with chaos and our hearts with love. Do you remember your first dog?

For as long as I can remember, dogs have been a huge part of my life. At one point during my childhood, my parents and I had six poodles. Let that sink in for a second—*six poodles!* I will say, every day was an adventure with those brilliant beauties, and we enjoyed every minute of it. When I was just a teenager, my parents and I joined our regional chapter of the Poodle Club of America and started educating ourselves on everything canine. We became close friends with groomers, breeders, rescuers, trainers, show handlers, pet product developers, and other dog lovers. I guess you can say we were obsessed.

As a woman who grew up with plenty of pups by her side, it's pretty obvious why when I packed my bags and moved across the country for a television news reporter job in my mid-twenties, I only made it two weeks before a dog was running around my apartment. Just the sight of a puppy

parent walking down the street with their fur baby's leash in hand made me miss my family dogs. So, I did what any normal canine-crazed person would do—I spent nearly every spare minute searching for a puppy. I went to various shelters and couldn't stop searching online. I even drove to meet a few dogs until one day I finally found *the one*. You know that feeling when you finally meet the perfect pooch, right? You just kind of look into each other's eyes and something clicks. I'm guessing you felt that same connection when you first met your pooch. Today, I'm blessed to say that I'm the proud dog mom to a Chihuahua, Diego, and toy Poodle, Gigi.

While I grew up treating my dogs as close family members, and perhaps you did too, when I brought Diego and Gigi home, something was different. For the first time, I was solely responsible for their care. Not my family. Me. As a former news reporter, I'm a naturally curious person. The lessons I learned in my career started creeping into my dog parenting style. Meaning, my vet visits became full-fledged interviews, and my time on Google turned into a research project.

Reading various articles and studies that linked rising rates of dog diabetes, obesity, and cancer to poor diet, I immediately took a magnifying lens to the ingredients in my dogs' store-bought food and treats. What I found was shocking: potentially cancer-causing preservatives, controversial artificial coloring, scale-tipping sugars, and other ingredients I couldn't even pronounce. Turns out, the relatively "cheap" foods and treats many of us give to our four-legged loves can actually lead to some pretty expensive vet bills. I knew something needed to change. That's when I teamed up with my mom, Donna.

My mom—a registered nurse, avid home chef, and parent to two adorable canine kids—had this wild idea to ditch the store-bought stuff altogether and become dog chefs. I call it a "wild" idea since I had never heard of anyone taking the time to make their dogs homemade food and snacks. Until now. As more recalls and red-flags surrounding processed foods and commercial treats hit the internet, more puppy parents are taking matters into their own hands.

Despite living on two different sides of the country, my mom and I started researching ingredients together. If we were going to do this, we wanted to do it right. We wanted to know which flours were the easiest for our dogs to digest. Which protein sources should we use? What about herbs and spices—which ones could help boost the canine immune system and which should we stay far away from? Would using organic ingredients make a difference? What about healthy fat sources and Omega-3s? We had so many questions.

After a lot of digging around and interviewing canine experts, we took our prior baking knowledge and mixed it with our new dog nutrition knowledge. Before we knew it, we started whipping up custom creations for our canine kids. As a little boost to our egos, they were going nuts over their new treats—quickly gobbling them down and then looking for more. I know my

excitement may seem silly—after all, some dogs are perfectly content eating scraps out of the garbage. I will say, though, I feel like I'm raising the pickiest dogs on earth. Before I started baking treats, whenever I would extend my hand out to offer food, my pups would spend a good 15–20 seconds sniffing it with a skeptical look on their faces. If it wasn't to their liking, they would just turn around and walk away, leaving the food in my hand. Sound familiar? I never thought I would meet such picky dogs, but, just like humans, they have likes and dislikes too!

All of the recipes in this book have been canine approved. Confession: They're also human approved. Since they're made from nutrient-rich ingredients that you or I would eat—*think kale, spinach, salmon, chicken, turmeric, ginger, etc.*—we taste test everything. I must admit, they're actually pretty delicious *(my favorites are the Pumpkin Pie Paws on page 173)*!

As you flip through our collection of 60 treat recipes, you'll find a little something for all dietary needs and taste preferences. Do you want your dog eating gluten or grain-free? We've got you covered. Need to add more protein to your pup's diet? We have plenty of flourless, protein-packed recipes that you can whip up with ease. Frozen treats to help your pooch beat the heat? Yup, we've got that too. A little something to give your dog at the holiday table so he doesn't feel left out? We've included a whole holiday chapter to get your pooch in the spirit!

Don't worry if you're not a master chef. Sprinkled through each chapter, we've included some helpful baking tricks, tool suggestions, and nutrition tips. Just relax and have fun. If your dogs are anything like mine, you'll get a kick out of watching them wait near your feet as you pull a tray of treats out of the oven. It's amazing to see how much they love and appreciate a home-cooked snack.

Happy baking,
Melissa

Why Homemade?

When I tell people that I bake 100% of my dogs' treats, I get one of two responses. Either the person gets very interested and wants me to share some recipes with them *or* they look at me like a crazy dog lady who has way too much time on her hands. While I'm perfectly content being labeled the "crazy dog lady," I think it's important to set the record straight on that last part.

Even though there are still 24 hours in a day, it seems life is just getting busier for people. Between work, family, every-day responsibilities, and trying to squeeze in some recreation, you probably don't have a lot of "extra" time. I get that. But, honestly, if you have an hour to run to the pet store and pick up a pack of treats, you have an hour to bake them.

So how many treats will an hour of kitchen time give you? Well, it all depends on the recipe, the size of your cookie cutters, and how many treats you give your dogs. Personally, I use mini cookie cutters for my two small dogs and can get anywhere from 55–100 treats out of my biscuit recipes. Give me just 15 minutes, though, and I can mix up a whole week's worth of frozen snacks for my two fur kids. While it's going to be slightly different for everyone, the point is, don't let the fear of a time commitment stop you from providing your dog with a healthier snack option. After all, there are a lot of benefits to making homemade treats.

Control Ingredients

Preservatives, by-products, and cheap fillers…oh my! Have you ever read through the ingredient label of your store-bought dog treats? While some are definitely better than others, processed biscuits, jerky, and chews usually contain questionable ingredients that your dog is better off avoiding. This was something my family and I had no clue about until we had a couple of health scares and started digging into dog nutrition.

I look back at some of the snacks we used to feed our dogs and I just cringe. I remember as a little girl hopping into the car with my dad and driving down to this small-town pet shop to pick up dozens of rawhide bones. We couldn't wait to get home where we were greeted by a pack of happy dogs, anxiously waiting to sink their teeth into their tasty treat. Growing up, my dogs loved to slobber and chew on rawhides, and we never even thought to question whether they were healthy for our pups or not. We just assumed they were. But you know what they say about assuming. Today we know that rawhides are covered in chemicals, pose a choking risk, and are linked to intestinal blockages. My family found that last one out the hard way when, about a decade ago, my mom's toy Poodle

experienced intestinal bleeding from rawhides. Thankfully, little Tina survived and is still with us today. But there are a lot of dogs out there who aren't that lucky. Needless to say, I don't feed my Diego and Gigi rawhides.

That was health scare number one for my family. Number two happened when one of my close family member's dog developed a kidney disorder as a direct result of eating treats manufactured in China. Remember back to 2014/2015 when reports of toxic treats from China started flooding the news? Not only did the news station where I worked cover it, but my family was directly affected.

Have you ever experienced a health scare with your dog as a direct result of commercial treats? It sure is scary and makes you think twice about what you're feeding your canine cutie.

A big problem with commercial snacks is their questionable ingredients. Cheap fillers—like soy, meat meal, and corn—should be left out of your dog's diet.

Artificial colorings are another thing to watch for. While they certainly make treats look pretty, fake coloring and food dyes have been linked to a rainbow of health risks in both humans and animals. Some of the most talked-about risks include behavioral problems, hyperactivity, anxiety, allergies, and even cancer. I promise your dog doesn't care what color his treats are!

Did you know that many manufacturers also add corn syrup and sugar to dog treats to make them more palatable? My jaw dropped when I saw sugar listed as an ingredient in my former favorite chicken jerky strips. Just as it affects humans, sugar can also lead to obesity, diabetes, tooth decay, inflammation, and cancer in pets.

Of course, I can't forget to mention the various preservatives that coat commercial treats.

The worst part is, there's no way to remove all of those unwanted ingredients once the manufacturer puts them in there. Rather than saying, "Oh well," and tossing your pooch something you're uncomfortable with, just make them yourself.

With homemade treats, you get to control everything that's included *(or not)* in your pup's snacks—from a particular ingredient to the quality of that ingredient.

Speaking of quality, I personally like to include plenty of fresh fruits and vegetables in my dogs' treats because research shows big benefits from the extra vitamins and minerals. When I feed my canine kids fresh berries and greens, I always opt for organic because I don't want a bunch of pesticides sitting in their bellies. If 100% organic isn't in your budget, I encourage you to use the Dirty Dozen/Clean 15 list as a guide for when to buy organic. Additionally, if I'm making chicken treats, I opt for hormone-free chicken. When I use salmon, I go for wild-caught. These are all high-quality ingredients that you simply won't get from a low-grade, fake, processed treat.

Tailor to Your Dog's Dietary Needs

If your dog has a food intolerance or allergy then finding treats that fit Fido's dietary needs can be a daunting task. The top three most common food issues for dogs are caused by beef, wheat, and dairy—but the list doesn't end there. If your pooch suffers from pancreatitis, for example, they'll need to avoid fats like the plague. If your little one is diabetic, you'll want to watch out for carbs and sweeteners—even natural sweeteners like raw honey and maple syrup. Only you and your veterinarian know what your dog can handle. By baking homemade treats, you can easily avoid any ingredient your heart desires.

In this book, you'll find recipes for dogs who eat grains and dogs who don't;

the average dog who can tolerate healthy fats and the ones who can't; the dog who digests yogurt and cheese with ease and those who suffer from a severe case of lactose intolerance. You'll notice some of the recipes contain a moderate amount of natural sweeteners, such as organic honey or raw maple syrup. If your dog is sensitive to these ingredients, or you're just uncomfortable with them, feel free to eliminate. Remember—you now have full control over what winds up in your pup's mouth.

In certain cases, even if your dog isn't allergic or sensitive to a type of food, you may still want to avoid a particular ingredient because of your own dietary restrictions. If a puppy parent has Celiac disease, for example, they may want their pooch eating gluten-free just to keep their household free of the controversial sticky protein.

May Save You Money

I don't know about your spending habits, but throughout my many years of buying commercial dog treats, dropping $100 or more during a trip to the pet store was not uncommon. While a bag of treats here and a few bones there may not seem like a lot of money when you reach the checkout counter, all of those dollars add up. I've easily spent thousands each year on "cheap" treats.

If you're someone who already bakes, chances are you have a lot of the needed tools and ingredients in your kitchen right now. So, you may be able to whip up custom treat creations without dropping a dime.

The Dog Chef Pantry

When baking for dogs, it's extremely important to know which human foods they can and cannot eat. That's because the canine body processes many foods differently than ours do. Sure, an apple a day may still keep the veterinarian away, and a little ginger before car rides may still help ease motion sickness. But not all foods that we consider healthy benefit our canine kids. In fact, even small amounts of certain "healthy foods"—such as onions and grapes—can be deadly to dogs. That's why, in my kitchen, I'm very careful with what ingredients I add to my homemade snacks. I avoid cheap fillers, such as corn meal. You will never see me use even a pinch of refined sugar, a drop of food coloring, or a spoon of hydrogenated oil. I stay away from overly fatty bacon and creams. Plus, even if a particular ingredient is questionable, like garlic, I prefer to leave it out. There are far too many superfoods and nourishing ingredients out there to settle for something controversial. After all, why replace a potentially dangerous commercial treat ingredient with another questionable one from your home?

If you like to play around in the kitchen by customizing recipes and making your own unique creations then let this yes/no food list serve as your guide for picking out nourishing ingredients!

Know Your Dog & Check with Your Vet

While the ingredients mentioned in the following "yes" list are considered safe for most dogs, it's important to note that everyone's body—human and canine—is different. Only you and your vet know what your individual pooch can handle. If your dog is allergic or sensitive to a particular ingredient that I've included on the "yes" list, don't add it to your homemade treats. You can either swap it out or completely eliminate the ingredient from my recipes. While I cannot guarantee that a recipe will turn out if you deviate from the original directions, I'm always a fan of experimenting in the kitchen. So, play around and have some fun!

Another important note: If you're introducing a new ingredient into your dog's diet, do so slowly.

Yes Ingredients

APPLES

This popular fruit is high in essential nutrients, such as immune-boosting vitamin C, digestive-aiding fiber, and muscle-aiding potassium. While apples offer your pup many benefits, make sure to remove the core and seeds before feeding your canine cutie this super-fruit. That's because apple seeds contain amygdalin, a substance that converts into cyanide when crushed or chewed. Cyanide is poisonous to your pooch and can prevent the blood from carrying oxygen throughout the body.

ALMOND BUTTER

Almond butter is loaded with healthy fats, protein, vitamins, and minerals that help your dog's body thrive. When searching for the best almond butter in your local grocery or health food store, make sure to read the ingredient label carefully. Your almond butter shouldn't have any artificial sweeteners or refined sugar added to it. The only thing that should be included on the ingredient label is almonds. If you have a hard time finding almond butter made from just almonds *(you'd be surprised— this can be a difficult task)*, you can always make your own. I promise it doesn't take that long. Just toss some almonds into a high-quality blender, flip the switch to high, and blend until creamy. Voilà, you're left with all-natural almond butter!

BANANAS

Have you seen that viral video of a small dog holding and munching on a banana?

That dog is so adorable! Okay … back to bananas. This is another popular and easily accessible fruit that is sure to please your pup's taste buds and body. They contain potassium, fiber, and magnesium.

BLUEBERRIES

Not only are they delicious and turn your treats a pretty color, but blueberries are also loaded with antioxidants that protect your dog's body in more ways than one. Research shows antioxidants fight free radicals that damage cells and tissues. Plus, they've been proven to protect the brain from oxidative stress and fight against cancer.

BROCCOLI

Broccoli is a cruciferous veggie that provides a nice dose of fiber, protein, potassium, and plenty of immune-boosting vitamin C *(did you know broccoli contains more vitamin C than an orange?)*. I like to chop this powerhouse vegetable into little pieces before adding it to my homemade treats or serving it up straight.

CARROTS

On their own, carrots are a great snack for your dog. They're also one of my favorite ingredients to add to homemade treats. Shredded carrots add a subtle crunch, a naturally sweet flavor, and boost of essential nutrients to DIY dog biscuits. The orange veggie is rich in beta carotene and vitamin A, which are both beneficial for your dog's eye health.

CHEESE

Most dogs are cheese lovers and, as long as you feed cheese in moderation, it's viewed as a healthy snack. Cheese is high in protein, calcium, essential fatty acids, and several key vitamins. Of course, if your dog is lactose intolerant then you should avoid cheese. While the tasty food contains less lactose than a glass of cow's milk, it still does have the potentially digestive-upsetting sugar. So dogs with severe lactose intolerance can have an adverse reaction from even the smallest amount of cheese. Additionally, avoid very rich, fatty cheeses, as well as cheeses that contain herbs which are considered toxic to dogs.

CHIA SEEDS

While these flavorless seeds may be tiny, they sure are nutritionally mighty. They tout calcium, iron, magnesium, and Omega-3 fatty acids. Incorporating Omega-3's into your dog's diet is key since they fight inflammation and have been linked to improved heart health, boosted brain health, better digestion, elevated mood, strengthened immune system, and improved skin condition. Chia seeds have even been known to improve a dog's coat and ease joint pain in senior citizen canines. Since chia seeds expand once they hit liquid, make sure to either soak them first or use ground chia seeds. I personally buy a big tub of pre-ground chia seeds for my dog treat baking.

CHICKEN

Chicken is an affordable source of protein that most canines go crazy over. It also contains essential vitamins, minerals, fats, and amino acids. Before adding chicken to your homemade treats, I encourage you to always cut off the excess fat.

COCONUT OIL

This superfood has antiviral, antibacterial, and antimicrobial properties. It's also been linked to increased nutrient absorption, improved digestion, improved breath, and weight management. Along with adding some coconut oil to your dog's treats, you can also apply it topically to their paw pads and nose—it works great as a natural moisturizer.

EGGS

Eggs are easy for most dogs to digest and can help give your treats a nice protein boost. Plus, they're high in iron (which wards off anemia), folate, and vitamin A.

FLAXSEEDS

Adding a sprinkle of ground flaxseeds into your homemade treats is a great way to boost fiber and Omega-3 fatty acids.

GINGER

Ginger is a super-spice that's been used for its medicinal purposes for thousands of years. Just like with humans, it's been linked to improved digestion in dogs. It's believed to help soothe a dog's upset stomach, relieve nausea, and ease motion sickness. So, if your dog suffers from car sickness and you're planning a road trip, try giving your dog a little ginger treat beforehand. Additionally, ginger has anti-cancer properties.

GREEN BEANS

This popular green veggie is rich in key vitamins and minerals. The best part? While green beans can certainly boost your dog treat's nutritional value, they won't hike up the calorie count. That's why green beans are viewed as the perfect snack for

THE DOG CHEF PANTRY

obese canine kids. Serve them boiled or dehydrated.

KALE

Kale is a superfood that deserves a spot in both your and your dog's diet. Mixing a moderate amount of chopped kale into your homemade treats bumps up the nutritional value big time since kale is rich in vitamin C, vitamin A, and potassium. Plus, this leafy green does pack a little protein (2.9g per cup).

PEANUT BUTTER

Dogs go crazy over peanut butter because of its rich, creamy texture and delicious flavor. Aside from the taste, it's also really good for your pooch since peanut butter is loaded with healthy fats and protein. When picking out the perfect peanut butter to include in your homemade dog treats, make sure to read the label very carefully. Look for one that only has peanuts on the ingredient list and always avoid brands that use Xylitol to sweeten their peanut butter. Xylitol is incredibly toxic to dogs, which I will talk about on page 19.

PUMPKIN

Pumpkin is part of the squash family and known as a superfood for dogs. It's great for settling a dog's upset stomach and easing digestive troubles. Pumpkin is often fed to sick dogs as a way to ease constipation and relieve bouts of diarrhea. These digestive benefits are thanks to the high fiber content. That's not the only way pumpkin can benefit Fido, though. Since it also contains protein, pumpkin can help keep your dog feeling full for longer. That means pumpkin can aid weight loss in an overweight pooch. It's important to note that when you see pumpkin listed in my recipes, I am not referring to pumpkin pie filling, which is loaded with sugar and spices that are toxic to dogs. Rather, I mean 100% Pure Pumpkin Purée.

SALMON

Sure, there are plenty of fish in the sea, but if you're looking to incorporate fish into your dog's diet then salmon is an excellent choice. Salmon is high in protein and Omega-3 fatty acids. If budget allows, opt for wild-caught over farm-raised fish *(which are pumped full of antibiotics)*. Additionally, before adding fresh salmon to your dog treats make sure the bones have been completely removed.

SPINACH

Please tell me when you eat spinach that you think of Popeye the Sailor Man too!

From a young age, we're taught that spinach is incredibly healthy for us. Well, thanks to its many vitamins, minerals, fiber, and protein, it's great for your fur baby too.

SPIRULINA

This blue-green "algae" is extremely rich in protein, key vitamins, and minerals. Thanks to its powerful nutrients, spirulina has been linked to decreasing inflammation, easing digestive issues, reducing arthritis symptoms, improving mental function, enhancing natural detoxification, and fighting cancer. While I do like to incorporate spirulina into my dog's treats, I feel it's important to mention that it's a rather expensive ingredient. If it's in your budget then try adding a ¼ teaspoon or so to one of my biscuit recipes. If not, you can easily leave this ingredient out.

STRAWBERRIES

Not only are strawberries delicious, they're also great for your pooch. Like blueberries, strawberries are rich in antioxidants that help fight free-radicals in the body, warding off various illnesses. Overtime, munching on this brightly colored berry can help strengthen your dog's immune system. So what's the best way to serve this fruit to your pup? Well, fresh is always best.

Avoid canned fruit or strawberries that are drenched in syrup. In my recipes, you will notice that I either cut my strawberries into tiny pieces or purée them before feeding them to my dogs. This will help eliminate possible choking hazards.

SWEET POTATOES

When I was a little kid, I only knew sweet potatoes as the orange stuff hidden underneath baked marshmallows on Thanksgiving. Turns out, that "orange stuff" is very healthy for both you and your dog (*the marshmallows—not so much*)! Today, I add unseasoned, peeled, cooked, and mashed sweet potatoes to many of my dogs' treats, and they love it. Adding sweet potato to your dog's existing diet provides a nice serving of fiber, key vitamins, and minerals.

TURMERIC

Turmeric is a yellow spice that's often used to flavor Indian cuisine. Along with its blasts of flavor, the powerful spice has been used for its medicinal purposes for centuries. Turmeric's therapeutic benefits are believed to be a result of its bioactive ingredient curcumin—*not to be confused with cumin*. It was widely used in traditional Chinese medicine as well as Ayurvedic medicine. Today, pet nutritionists recommend you give it to your pooch too. Similar to how it benefits humans, adding turmeric to your dog's diet is believed to help ward off cancer, fight inflammation, aid digestion, kill dangerous parasites, and even boost mood.

YOGURT

Plain yogurt is rich in probiotics, which improve gut health and aid digestion. Yogurt also provides calcium, protein, and healthy fats. When you see yogurt listed in my recipes, I'm referring to a plain yogurt that contains live cultures. Always avoid yogurts that contain artificial sweeteners, added sugar, or artificial flavors.

ZUCCHINI

Zucchini is a type of squash that can be eaten either raw or cooked. While it's 95 percent water, zucchini packs a nutritional punch and is extremely beneficial to your dog's health.

No Ingredients

ALCOHOL

Your pooch doesn't need to party like a rockstar. No amount of alcohol is safe for canines and you should never leave an unattended glass of wine, beer, or liquor around your four-legged family member. If your dog does drink alcohol, ethanol will be absorbed into his system. It's important to understand that a dog's metabolism can't process ethanol like yours can. Your pooch will likely get drunk and experience symptoms such as confusion, lack of coordination, difficulty breathing, and even seizures. If your dog consumes alcohol on an empty stomach you may notice these symptoms as quickly as 30 minutes. If your dog is drunk, call your vet immediately. He will probably need to be treated with activated charcoal to absorb the toxins and put on IV therapy for hydration.

CHOCOLATE

While most people know that chocolate is toxic to dogs, you may be surprised to find out how many dogs still get their paws on the sweet stuff. Theobromine and caffeine are two compounds in chocolate that stimulate the nervous system, causing severe symptoms.

COFFEE AND TEA

Caffeine is the culprit here and you want to keep it away from your pooch. Keep the coffee grounds and tea bags away from Fido and out of their homemade treat doughs because they are extremely sensitive to its effects. Many of us wake up and the first thing we want to do is grab a cup of coffee to kick-start our day. Caffeine is a stimulant, and, with that said, it makes sense that some symptoms of caffeine poisoning or caffeine overdose in our fur kids would be hyperactivity, increased heart rate, shaking, vomiting, possible seizures, collapse, or unconsciousness.

GRAPES

While it hasn't been identified as to what the exact toxin is that makes grapes dangerous for dogs, it is well documented that even small amounts of grapes and raisins can cause kidney failure and death.

MACADAMIA NUTS

It's unknown what causes the toxic effects of macadamia nuts in dogs, but it's well-established that eating the nut can cause dogs to exhibit symptoms within 12 hours of ingestion. Symptoms can include vomiting, fatigue, muscle weakness, difficulty walking, depression, tremors, joint stiffness, and increased body temperature. The high fat content can also cause pancreatitis.

ONIONS, GARLIC, CHIVES & LEEKS

Onions are highly toxic to dogs and can cause hemolytic anemia, which is damage to a dog's red blood cells and can cause them to rupture/burst. Onions, garlic, chives, and leeks are all part of the Allium family. Some like to argue that garlic is fine for dogs in small to moderate amounts. Your vet may have even recommended it for medicinal purposes. There are pros and cons to its use. Since there is controversy surrounding garlic, though, you will never see it listed as an ingredient in my recipes.

PITS AND SEEDS FROM FRUIT

Many fruit pits and seeds are known to contain a compound that breaks down into cyanide when ingested. Cyanide is toxic to dogs. Additionally, pits and seeds can pose a choking hazard and/or cause an intestinal blockage. In general, if a fruit contains pits or seeds, avoid them.

POTATO SKINS (RAW)

Raw potatoes can be harsh on the stomach. Plus, raw potato skins (as well as under-ripened potatoes) can contain solanine, which is a glycoalkaloid poison. It can affect your pooch's nervous system and gastrointestinal system. Solanine poisoning can be deadly.

SALT

I think most of us are guilty of sharing a salty chip or pretzel with our pooches. With that said, if your dog does indulge in the occasional salty treat, don't overdo it. Salt is actually something that your canine kid can, and should, do without. First of all, salty foods will make him thirsty. Second, an excess of salt can actually lead to sodium poisoning and can be life-threatening.

SUGAR

Similar to how sugar affects humans, it has been linked to diabetes, heart disease, obesity, and even cancer in canines. For these reasons, I never include refined sugar in my dog treats, and I keep natural sweeteners to a minimum. Remember, sugar is sugar no matter what form it's in.

WALNUTS

Nuts in general should be a "no go" food for your pooch since most have a high fat content. High dietary fat in dogs can lead to pancreatitis, which can be fatal. Many nuts are difficult for dogs to digest and can be an intestinal obstruction hazard.

XYLITOL

While this naturally-derived sweetener alternative is commonly used in sugar-free foods and considered safe for humans, it's extremely toxic to dogs. If your pooch consumes even a small amount of xylitol, it could lead to a steep drop in blood sugar, liver damage, and even death. If you think that your dog has eaten xylitol, it's critical to see a vet or animal ER immediately. In as little as 30-60 minutes, the effects of xylitol can be deadly.

YEAST DOUGH

Yeast dough refers to unbaked bread dough, and it can harm your pooch in a couple of ways. When yeast dough sits in a dog's stomach, it can expand due to the warm and moist environment. This can cause stomach upset, bloat, twisting of the stomach, or even death. Additionally, the yeast dough can ferment in the stomach, which morphs into alcohol and carbon dioxide. The alcohol can become toxic very quickly as it's rapidly absorbed into the dog's G.I. tract.

The Flours You'll Find in Proud Dog Mom Recipes

ALMOND FLOUR

Almond flour is made from blanched (skinned) almonds that are finely ground into flour. When shopping for almond flour, you'll notice there are various grounds. You will also likely come across bags that say "Almond Meal" on them. Almond meal is similar to almond flour, but it's coarser and the skins are generally left on. While almond meal is considered safe for dogs, when flipping through this cookbook, I am referring to a fine ground almond flour. I find the finer the flour, the better the biscuit texture. Almond flour is both gluten and grain-free.

BROWN RICE FLOUR
Brown rice flour is simply ground up grain brown rice. Adding it to your dog biscuits will give them a mild nutty flavor that works well with vegetables, various meats, and cheese. Brown rice flour is gluten-free.

BUCKWHEAT FLOUR
A lot of people assume buckwheat contains wheat because of the name. But this wheat-free flour is actually made from a fruit seed that's related to rhubarb! It's high in protein, fiber, and various vitamins. Plus, it's relatively low in carbohydrates and has practically no fat. Buckwheat flour offers a bold, nutty flavor and is gluten-free and grain-free.

COCONUT FLOUR
Coconut flour is made from dried coconut meat. It's high in fiber, protein, and healthy fats. Adding coconut flour to your homemade biscuits will give them a slight coconut flavor, which most dogs seem to love. Coconut flour is naturally gluten-free and grain-free.

GARBANZO BEAN FLOUR
Made from ground up chickpeas, this flour is high in protein and gives treats a rich taste. Garbanzo bean flour is naturally gluten-free and grain-free.

OAT FLOUR
Made from ground-up oats, oat flour can be purchased from your local grocery/health food store or made at home. To make your own oat flour, simply grab some quick oats and toss them into a food processor. Grind them until they become a fine flour. While you may feel compelled to stop grinding the oats after just a minute or two, I recommend to keep processing them for about five minutes, or until they no longer have a grainy texture. To ensure you've ground the oats fine enough, use a sifter and eliminate any large chunks that remain. Oat flour is naturally gluten-free.

QUINOA FLOUR

Made from ground up quinoa *(which is a seed that's related to spinach, beets, and chard)*, this is another type of flour that is simple to make at home. Just toast the quinoa seeds in a dry skillet until they begin to brown and pop, then transfer to a food processor. It should only take about a minute or two to grind this high-protein seed into a flour. To ensure your homemade quinoa flour is fine enough, use a sifter. I personally like to run my homemade quinoa flour through the sifter twice and eliminate any large chunks that remain. Similar to brown rice flour, I like to use quinoa flour with various vegetables, lean meats, and cheese. This type of flour is naturally gluten and grain-free.

TAPIOCA FLOUR (AKA TAPIOCA STARCH)

Made from the dried roots of a cassava plant, this starchy and lightly sweet flour is the perfect thickening agent. That's exactly why you'll find this ingredient listed in all of my icing recipes. Tapioca flour is naturally gluten and grain-free.

Make Baking a Breeze

When it comes to successful baking, there are a lot of different variables that come into play. You can have 10 dog moms follow the same recipe and it may come out 10 different ways. Someone's treats may come out of the oven dry and cracked, while someone else's may end up wet and soggy. One puppy parent's dough may yield 75 biscuits while another's may yield 110. It happens.

The most important thing is to not get frustrated. A recipe can almost always be fixed. If a treat dough seems dry, simply add more liquid a tablespoon at a time. If a dough is too sticky to work with, add more flour about a ¼ cup at a time *(unless the recipe directions state the dough is supposed to be sticky and tells you how to work with it).* Are your flour-based biscuits cracking and bowing? Take a look at your oven temperature—it may be too high. Are your biscuits too soft in the middle? You probably didn't bake them long enough. Again, there is almost always a simple fix—it's just a matter of figuring out the problem.

Throughout my time baking dog treats, the following kitchen tools and measuring tips have helped me greatly. Now creating homemade dog snacks in my kitchen has become sort of like a well-oiled machine. When I re-make a recipe, it comes out the same way every time. You will get into a groove too!

The Tools for Success

OVEN THERMOMETER

I'm starting with an oven thermometer because this is as basic as it gets. If you want bark-worthy baked goods then you have to know your oven is baking at the correct temperature. Seems like a no-brainer, right!? Just set the oven to the temperature you want and after it preheats … bake. Unfortunately, unless you've recently had your oven calibrated and tested, chances are your temperature is not as accurate as you think. Without an oven thermometer, you'll have no way of knowing. In fact, when I first started baking for this book, I went through a really strange two-day period where I burned literally every single treat that I baked. Despite baking at my usual 350°F, when I pulled batch after batch out of the oven, I was left with dark brown, severely cracked, and bowed messes. After giving it some thought, I picked up an oven thermometer. I put it in the oven, set it to 350°, and just 10 minutes later the thermometer shot up to 400°. Yes, 50° above my setting! I let it go for a little longer and it didn't come down. I turned off the oven, let it cool, started over, and got the same result. I've since moved and my new oven hits the correct temperature every time. But the point is, everyone's oven is different, and I encourage you to use an oven thermometer to ensure accuracy.

MIXING BOWLS

I recommend having small, medium, and large bowls on hand for mixing your biscuit and pupcake doughs.

MEASURING CUPS

These are a must for accurate measuring. There are two types that you should have on hand. The first type is better for dry ingredients—it's an actual cup with a handle and rim, so you can fill it all the way up and then level off. You will use this type of measuring cup to measure ingredients such as flour, fruits, veggies, and herbs. They normally come in sets of four cups with measuring sizes of ¼ cup, ⅓ cup, ½ cup, and 1 cup. The second type is a clear cup that looks like a small pitcher. It has a spout for pouring liquids and has marked measurements for cups, ounces, and milliliters on the side. This type of measuring cup comes in various sizes, but for the purpose of baking dog treats, I would recommend having a 2-cup size.

MEASURING SPOONS

These are also a must-have for accurate measurements. You will use them to measure spices like ground ginger, turmeric, and spirulina. Measuring spoons come in sets, and the standard measuring amounts are ¼ teaspoon, ½ teaspoon, 1 teaspoon, and 1 tablespoon. Some sets will also include ⅛ teaspoon, ½ tablespoon, and 1½ tablespoon measure, which really come in handy.

WHISK

When I'm baking biscuits, I generally start out by adding my dry ingredients to a bowl and then mixing them together with a whisk to ensure everything is thoroughly combined. While you can certainly get away with not using a whisk, it's nice to have one on hand!

GRATER

Throughout many of my recipes, you will see I call for grated fruits and vegetables. I definitely recommend picking up a grater that features a comfortable hand grip. Trust me, after several minutes of sliding your carrots, zucchini, and apples up and down the rough surface of a grater, your hands can get pretty tired! I personally have a multi-sided grater, which allows me to choose how fine I want my ingredients shredded.

ROLLING PIN

When it comes to rolling pins, you have a lot of choices—wood, plastic, silicone, and marble. Some have handles, some are tapered on the ends, and some are plain cylinders. I personally like a rolling pin with handles. But, no matter what style of rolling pin you choose, it will make rolling and flattening your dough balls a real breeze.

BAKING SHEETS OR COOKIE SHEETS

A cookie sheet is a flat sheet of metal—normally made of aluminum or stainless steel—and has a curved rim on one end of the pan. Baking sheets have a rimmed edge around all four sides and are also known as jelly roll pans. Both are perfect for baking flat items like dog biscuits and cookies. Whichever type you prefer to use, I would suggest having two on hand since many treat recipes in this book will give you enough dough to fill two pans.

PARCHMENT PAPER

Parchment paper will become your best friend when baking dog biscuits. It provides a non-stick surface and easy cleanup. When rolling out dog treat biscuit doughs, I usually lay one piece of parchment paper on the counter and another piece of parchment paper on top of the dough ball. Then, I roll my dough ball flat with a rolling pin. That second sheet of parchment paper helps to keep my rolling pin clean and also keeps me sane when rolling sticky doughs.

BAKING MAT

One thing you will notice when following the parchment paper sandwich method that I outlined in the previous tool suggestion is the bottom piece of parchment paper easily slides on the countertop. My solution? Place a silicone baking mat underneath to provide a non-slip surface. So, I don't personally use my baking mat in the oven. But it does come in handy when rolling dough and prepping biscuits!

COOLING RACKS

When your treats come out of the oven, it's best to transfer them to a cooling rack so air can circulate around your baked goods and speed up the cooling process.

SILICONE MOLDS

I recently started collecting silicone molds because I get a lot of use out of them. I use them for pupcakes, flourless quiches, puppy frittatas, and frozen treats. My favorites are my paw print and bone molds, as you can probably guess after flipping through this book. Have fun and play around with molds, though. You may even want to use fun festive molds during the holiday season.

MINI MUFFIN TIN

If you don't want to use a silicone mold—or don't have one handy—you can always use a mini-muffin tin instead. I prefer the mini size because I have small dogs, but use whichever size you prefer.

COOKIE CUTTERS

I remember the first time I baked dog biscuits with a cookie cutter and, wow, was I impressed! Bones, paws, fire hydrants, stars, circles, hearts, and the list goes on. Truly, all you really need is one, but cookie cutters are kind of like potato chips—I bet you'll want more than one!

FOOD PROCESSOR

A food processor will help you rough chop ingredients and is going to come in handy for a few reasons. First, if you plan to make your own flours then you are going to need a food processor to grind your ingredients. Second, if you don't have the time or patience to finely chop various veggies and herbs included in some of the biscuit recipes, you can always throw them into a food processor and pulse a few times.

BLENDER

While a food processor rough chops, you'll use a blender to purée ingredients. Throughout this book, you'll come across recipes that call for puréeing fruits, vegetables, and sometimes even meats. You'll get use out of your blender when making some biscuits, along with recipes in the Burgers and Bites, Pupsicles, and Icing chapters.

SIFTER

If you're planning on making your own flours—like oat and quinoa flours—then a sifter will ensure your ingredients are fine enough.

Measuring Tips

FLOUR

When measuring flour, a lot of people have the urge to take their measuring cup, stick it in the flour bag, and scoop. Does that sound familiar? While it may be the easiest way to gather a cup of flour, it won't leave you with an accurate measurement. Rather, scooping leaves you with way too much flour. Instead, when following the recipes in this book *(and most cookbooks unless otherwise stated)* you'll want to use the "spoon and level" method:

- 🐾 Take a spoon and fluff up the flour so it is no longer compacted in the bag or canister.
- 🐾 Spoon the flour into a dry measuring cup until it reaches a little above the top. Do not compact it, tap it, or press it down. Just leave it fluffy.
- 🐾 Use the back of a knife to level off the flour.

OATS

While I generally use oat flour in my dog treat recipes, you may come across some recipes that require whole oats. Whether you are using whole oats or quick oats, you will still use the "spoon and level" method.

PEANUT BUTTER, APPLESAUCE, PUMPKIN PURÉE (& OTHER SEMI-LIQUID INGREDIENTS)

These ingredients add a lot of flavor to your dog's homemade treats *(they also add extra nutrients, like we talked about in The Dog Chef Pantry section)*! When measuring peanut butter, applesauce, pumpkin purée, or any other semi-liquid ingredients, you'll want to use your dry measuring cups. Again, use the spoon and level method. Then use a rubber spatula (or another utensil you have on hand) to help release the ingredient.

HONEY & MAPLE SYRUP

Measuring honey and maple syrup is simple. Just pour your syrup into a measuring spoon. Then, use the back of a knife to level your sweetener if it's very thick and heaping. Use a small rubber baking spatula to scoop all of the honey or maple syrup out of the measuring spoon and into your mixing bowl.

LIQUID INGREDIENTS

When baking homemade dog treats, I often use either water, coconut water, or homemade chicken broth as my liquid. Rather than using a dry measuring cup, you'll want to use a clear liquid measuring cup — that's the one that looks like a small pitcher with a spout for pouring liquids. On the side of this type of measuring cup, you will see marked graduated measurements for cups, ounces, and milliliters. The advantage of this cup for liquids is the extra room in it. You can fill your liquid ingredients up to the desired measurement without worrying it will spill over. To properly measure your liquid:

- Place the cup on the counter.
- Bend down so that you can read the cup markings at eye level.

- Fill the cup with liquid until it reaches your desired marking.

With proper measuring, awareness of your oven temperature, and an understanding of how to adjust a recipe if needed, you are on your way to dog treat success. I bet your pup is already drooling and licking his chops!

Storage Tips

Paired with each recipe in this book, you'll find tips to store your new preservative-free treat creations. As a general rule, make sure your treats are totally cooled before attempting to pack and store them in an airtight container. Now let's talk about how long they'll actually last. The drier and crisper your treat, the longer the shelf life. Softer treats and pupcakes tend to spoil sooner at room temperature, so store them in the fridge. You see, moistness can promote mold at a quicker rate. Also, take notice of the ingredients in your treats. If you have fresh fruits, vegetables, eggs, dairy, or anything that you would consider perishable, refrigerate. That's not to mention environmental conditions. If you live in a hot and humid region then your treats won't last quite as long on the counter compared to a cooler and drier climate. If you're making large quantities of biscuits, freezing them in an airtight container usually works great, and most of the treats in this book can be stored for up to three months in the freezer.

Gluten-Free Biscuits

The Recipes

The Basic Biscuit

I call this biscuit "The Basic Biscuit" because it's easy to make and super simple to customize, as you'll see by my variations on the next few pages. Follow the recipe as is or add your favorite dog-approved spices, chopped herbs, or shredded veggies. This recipe works particularly well when paired with other sweet ingredients since the biscuit naturally lends itself to a sweeter flavor. That's thanks to the combination of oat flour, coconut flour, and coconut oil. A quick note on the coconut oil—you may notice stores carry it in both solid and liquid states. When I list this superfood as an ingredient in my recipes, I'm referring to an unrefined, virgin coconut oil that is solid at room temperature and liquid when above 76°F. You see, while both products are labeled as coconut oil, they're not exactly the same. Rather, those bottles of liquefied coconut oil have undergone extra processing, eliminating some of the beneficial fatty acids (*find out more about how to choose the best coconut oil on page 127*).

INGREDIENTS:

3 cups oat flour

1 cup coconut flour

2 large eggs

1 cup water

¼ cup coconut oil

NOTES:

🐾 Are the center of your biscuits softer than you'd like? Instead of removing them from the oven, simply turn the oven off, crack the door open, and let the biscuits cool right inside. They will continue to dry out in the gradually fading heat. *Watch carefully to ensure they don't burn.*

🐾 Store in an airtight container in the refrigerator up to three weeks or in the freezer up to three months.

DIRECTIONS:

1 Preheat oven to 350°F.

2 Line two baking sheets with parchment paper. Set aside.

3 Add oat and coconut flours to a large mixing bowl. Whisk together until thoroughly combined.

4 Make a well in the center of the flours, add remaining ingredients, and mix with a spoon or fork.

5 With your hands, knead dough for several minutes, eventually forming a dough ball.

6 Sandwich dough ball between two sheets of parchment paper and roll flat (about ¼" thick) with a rolling pin.

7 Using a cookie cutter, stamp out biscuits.

8 Place biscuits on parchment paper-lined baking sheet and bake for 25–30 minutes.

9 Transfer biscuits to a wire rack to cool.

Kale & Spinach Cookies

Kale and spinach are a powerhouse combo. The two veggies are often called *superfoods* because, while they're low in calories, they're loaded with various vitamins and minerals that benefit both you and your pooch. The greens have been known to fight inflammation and boost the immune system (just to name a few benefits). This variation of The Basic Biscuit (page 33) is a great way to squeeze a few extra greens into your dog's diet. When you're chopping your veggies, make sure to keep going until they're super fine. The larger the veggie bits, the tougher it will be to stamp out your cookies with the cookie cutter. If you have a hard time chopping them with a knife, you can always toss your greens into a food processor and pulse a few times. Just make sure not to over-process, because you don't want to purée the greens!

INGREDIENTS:

3 cups oat flour

1 cup coconut flour

½ cup kale leaves

½ cup spinach leaves

2 large eggs

1 cup water

¼ cup coconut oil

NOTES:

 Are the center of your biscuits softer than you'd like? Instead of removing them from the oven, simply turn the oven off, crack the door open, and let the biscuits cool right inside. They will continue to dry out in the gradually fading heat. *Watch carefully to ensure they don't burn.*

Store in airtight container in the refrigerator for one week or in the freezer up to three months.

DIRECTIONS:

1   Preheat oven to 350°F.

2   Line two baking sheets with parchment paper. Set aside.

3   Add oat and coconut flours to a large mixing bowl. Whisk together until thoroughly combined.

4   Finely chop kale and spinach. You can either use a knife or pulse the veggies in a food processor. Add to mixing bowl and whisk.

5   Make a well in the center of the dry ingredients and add remaining wet ingredients. Mix together with a spoon or fork.

6   With your hands, knead dough for several minutes, eventually forming a dough ball.

7   Sandwich dough ball between two sheets of parchment paper and roll flat (about ¼" thick) with a rolling pin.

8   Using a cookie cutter of your choice, stamp out biscuits.

9   Place biscuits on a parchment paper-lined baking sheet and bake for 25–30 minutes.

10 Transfer biscuits to a wire rack to cool.

Fresh Breath Biscuits

Are you ever overwhelmed by the odor coming from your pooch's mouth? Don't be embarrassed to say yes—bad breath in dogs is very common. While I definitely recommend brushing your dog's teeth to tackle the root of the problem—*plaque, tarter, and bacteria*—you can also toss your fur kid one of these puppy-approved breath mint biscuits. This variation of The Basic Biscuit (page 33) includes odor-fighting mint and parsley leaves. Plus, the coconut oil touts anti-bacterial properties, making it great for oral health. Of course, your canine cutie doesn't have to have stinky breath to enjoy these homemade biscuits—it's just an added benefit!

INGREDIENTS:

3 cups oat flour

1 cup coconut flour

¼ cup fresh parsley leaves

¼ cup fresh mint leaves

2 large eggs

1 cup water

¼ cup coconut oil

NOTES:

 Are the center of your biscuits softer than you'd like? Instead of removing them from the oven, simply turn the oven off, crack the door open, and let the biscuits cool right inside. They will continue to dry out in the gradually fading heat. *Watch carefully to ensure they don't burn.*

Store in airtight container in the refrigerator for one week or in the freezer up to three months.

DIRECTIONS:

1 Preheat oven to 350°F.

2 Line two baking sheets with parchment paper. Set aside.

3 Add oat and coconut flours to a mixing bowl. Whisk together until thoroughly combined. Set aside.

4 Finely chop parsley and mint leaves— just the leaves, avoid the stems. You can either use a knife or pulse the herbs in a food processor. Add to mixing bowl and whisk together.

5 Make a well in the center of the dry ingredients and add remaining wet ingredients. Mix together with a spoon or fork.

6 With your hands, knead dough for several minutes, eventually forming a dough ball.

7 Sandwich dough ball between two sheets of parchment paper and roll flat (about ¼" thick) with a rolling pin.

8 Using a cookie cutter, stamp out biscuits.

9 Place biscuits on a parchment paper-lined baking sheet and bake for 25–30 minutes.

10 Transfer biscuits to a wire rack to cool.

How to Roll Dough Like a Pro

In the first few recipes of this cookbook, and the recipes that fill the chapters to come, you will probably notice that I recommend sandwiching your biscuit dough balls between two pieces of parchment paper before rolling them out flat with a rolling pin. This trick is a major lifesaver when working with either sticky doughs or drier doughs. With that said, I use this method every time I roll out a dog biscuit dough ball. Why? Well, there are a few reasons:

1   Some bakers dust their work surface and rolling pin with flour before rolling out their dough to prevent the mixture from sticking. However, the parchment paper sandwich method eliminates the need to use extra flour. Trust me, when you're working with rather expensive flours, like almond flour, it's a shame to waste even a little bit.
2   It keeps the rolling pin clean, meaning less cleanup for you.
3   It keeps the dough surface smooth, which usually translates into prettier treats.

Here is a quick photo guide to rolling out your dough balls (Extra tip: I like to place a baking mat underneath my first sheet of parchment paper to prevent it from sliding on the countertop).

Rice & Beans Biscuit

Okay … so this biscuit doesn't actually have whole rice or beans in it. It's made with a combination of brown rice flour and garbanzo bean flour *(AKA chickpea flour)*—but the name sounded like a good one for this treat! The shredded carrots give these bones a sweet flavor and the finely chopped parsley leaves offer up a hint of freshness. My favorite part about these bones—and my dogs' favorite part too—is the crunchy texture. So, toss one to your pooch and standby with open ears. *Oh, the sound of dogs happily eating is a satisfying one, don't you agree?!*

INGREDIENTS:

1½ cups brown rice flour
1½ cups garbanzo bean flour
¾ cup peeled and finely grated carrots
2 tablespoons finely chopped parsley leaves
1 large egg
3 tablespoons water

NOTES:

* Be careful not to pack carrots when measuring or dough will become too wet and sticky.
* This dough is stiffer than many of my other recipes. To make rolling easier, I usually separate the dough ball in half and then flatten separately.
* Store in airtight container in the refrigerator for one-two weeks or in the freezer up to three months.

DIRECTIONS:

1   Preheat oven to 350°F.
2   Line two baking sheets with parchment paper. Set aside.
3   In a large mixing bowl, add brown rice and garbanzo bean flours. Whisk together.
4   Make a well in the center of the flours and add carrots, parsley, egg, and water. Mix with a spoon or fork.
5   With your hands, knead the dough, working the wet ingredients into the flours. The mixture will be dry at first and then a little sticky. Keep kneading the dough for a few minutes until you get a Play Doh-like consistency.
6   Sandwich dough ball between two sheets of parchment paper and roll flat (about ¼" thick) with a rolling pin.
7   Using a cookie cutter, stamp out biscuits.
8   Place biscuits on baking sheet.
9   Bake 23–25 minutes.
10 Transfer biscuits to a wire rack to cool.

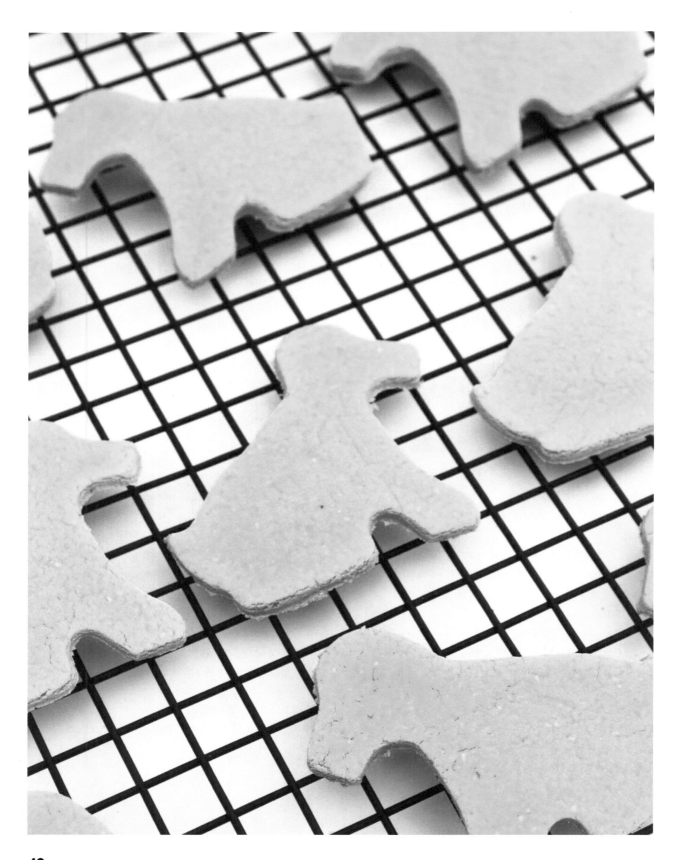

Pumpkin Apple Pooches

Stressed out? Whip up a batch of these biscuits because the soft and easily moldable dough is very satisfying to knead—just like a stress ball, but your dog will benefit! As you read through the ingredients, you will see applesauce listed. If you're using store-bought applesauce—which is what I use—then make sure to read the ingredient label carefully. Most jars of applesauce are loaded with sugar and some are flavored with spices. While those may please your palate when spooning some onto the side of your dinner dish, when incorporating applesauce into your homemade dog biscuits, you want to look for a brand that is solely made from apples and nothing else—no sugar, no artificial sweeteners, no cinnamon, no nutmeg, no lemon juice, etc. Just apples! I usually get mine from my local health food store and pick up a few bottles at a time so I can share it with the pups. Once these biscuits are fully baked, they'll be super crunchy on the outside and offer a touch of cookie-like softness in the middle.

INGREDIENTS:

3 cups brown rice flour

1 cup oat flour

½ cup 100% pure pumpkin purée

½ cup all-natural applesauce

½ cup water

NOTES:

 Store in airtight container in the refrigerator for one-two weeks or in the freezer up to three months.

DIRECTIONS:

1 Preheat oven to 350°F.

2 Line two baking sheets with parchment paper. Set aside.

3 In a large mixing bowl, add brown rice and oat flours. Whisk together.

4 Make a well in the center of the flours and add pumpkin purée, applesauce, and water. Mix with a spoon or fork.

5 With your hands, knead dough for several minutes, eventually forming a dough ball.

6 Sandwich dough ball between two sheets of parchment paper and roll flat (about ¼" thick) with a rolling pin.

7 Using a cookie cutter, stamp out biscuits.

8 Place biscuits on baking sheet.

9 Bake 25–30 minutes.

10 Transfer biscuits to a wire rack to cool.

Peanut Butter Ginger Snaps

As you're making the dough for these canine-approved ginger snap cookies, a yummy smell of peanut butter will fill the air. After they're baked all the way through and your pup bites down, the hint of ginger and cinnamon will come through. The blend of flavors and nice crunchy texture is one dogs go crazy for. Now a quick tip for you—the dog chef. If you keep your peanut butter in the fridge, let it sit out on your counter for about 10-15 minutes before measuring and adding it to your dough so it warms up a bit. I find cold peanut butter more difficult to massage into my dough ball. In a pinch for time? You can always pop the peanut butter in the microwave for 15 seconds to soften.

INGREDIENTS:

3 cups brown rice flour

1 cup oat flour

1 teaspoon ginger

½ teaspoon cinnamon

1 cup water

½ cup 100% pure pumpkin purée

⅓ cup organic peanut butter

NOTES:

 These treats will come out of the oven burning hot, so be careful when transferring them to your cooling rack.

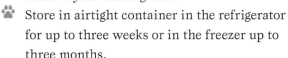 Store in airtight container in the refrigerator for up to three weeks or in the freezer up to three months.

DIRECTIONS:

1   Preheat oven to 350°F.

2   Line two baking sheets with parchment paper. Set aside.

3   In a large mixing bowl, add brown rice flour, oat flour, ginger, and cinnamon. Whisk together.

4   Make a well in the center of your dry ingredients and add water, pumpkin purée, and peanut butter. Mix together with a spoon or fork.

5   With your hands, knead dough for several minutes, eventually forming a dough ball.

6   Sandwich dough ball between two sheets of parchment paper and roll flat (about ¼" thick) with a rolling pin.

7   Using a cookie cutter, stamp out biscuits.

8   Place biscuits on baking sheet.

9   Bake 30 minutes.

10 Transfer biscuits to a wire rack to cool. When you first remove the treats from the oven, they will seem a bit softer in the middle than around the edges. As the treats cool, they will harden and crunch up.

Blue Bones

Blueberries are rich in antioxidants and have been known to help boost brain health, fight cancer cells, benefit heart health, and combat aging. Plus, they're downright delicious! Since blueberries pack so much goodness, I'm always looking for new ways to work them into my dogs' food. But, to be honest, when I first made these bones, I was a little worried my dogs would grab one, run over to my white rug, and then leave a big blue stain. After all, they're loaded with fresh blueberry juice. I'm happy to report, though, once these blue bones are fully baked, they shouldn't run or stain!

INGREDIENTS:

1½ cups brown rice flour

1 cup oat flour

¾ cup fresh blueberries

1 large egg

2 tablespoons water

2 tablespoons coconut oil

NOTES:

 Store in airtight container in the refrigerator for one-two weeks or in the freezer up to three months.

DIRECTIONS:

1   Preheat oven to 350°F.

2   Line two baking sheets with parchment paper. Set aside.

3   In a large mixing bowl, add brown rice and oat flours. Whisk together.

4   In a blender, purée blueberries.

5   Make a well in the center of your flour and add puréed blueberries, egg, water, and coconut oil. Mix together with a spoon or fork.

6   With your hands, knead dough for several minutes, eventually forming a dough ball.

7   Sandwich dough ball between two sheets of parchment paper and roll flat (about ¼" thick) with a rolling pin.

8   Using a cookie cutter, stamp out biscuits.

9   Place biscuits on baking sheet.

10   Bake 25–30 minutes, or until the edges become golden.

11   Transfer biscuits to a wire rack to cool.

48

Cheesy Smile Bones

Does your dog love cheese? If so, he'll love these bark-worthy biscuits that are loaded with shredded cheddar cheese! To elevate these cheesy bones even higher on your dog's snack wish list, I've paired them with a moderate amount of all-natural applesauce. You can think of it like a cheese and apple snack for human kids, but in biscuit form for your four-legged fur ball!

INGREDIENTS:

3 cups brown rice flour
1 cup oat flour
½ cup shredded cheddar cheese
2 large eggs
½ cup all-natural applesauce
⅓ cup water

NOTES:

 Store in airtight container in the refrigerator up to one week or in the freezer up to one month.

DIRECTIONS:

1 Preheat oven to 350°F.
2 Line two baking sheets with parchment paper. Set aside.
3 In a large mixing bowl, add brown rice flour, oat flour, and cheddar cheese. Whisk together.
4 In a separate bowl, beat eggs.
5 Add applesauce and water to eggs and thoroughly combine.
6 Add wet ingredients to dry ingredients and mix with a spoon or fork.
7 With your hands, knead dough for several minutes, eventually forming a dough ball.
8 Let dough rest in freezer for 15 minutes.
9 Sandwich dough ball between two sheets of parchment paper and roll flat (about ¼" thick) with a rolling pin.
10 Using a cookie cutter, stamp out biscuits.
11 Place biscuits on baking sheet.
12 Bake 30 minutes.
13 Transfer biscuits to a wire rack to cool.

How to Half a Recipe

Want to make a fresh snack for your canine companion, but dreading the thought of having upwards of 100 preservative-free biscuits lying around? Since the recipes in this cookbook don't have any preservatives, their shelf life isn't nearly as long as the commercial biscuits you buy at the pet store. Many only last a week or two in the fridge. Sure, you could simply pop your extra treats in the freezer, but there's another solution. Just half the recipe!

1 cup	=	½ cup		¼ cup	=	2 tablespoons
¾ cup	=	6 tablespoons		1 tablespoon	=	1½ teaspoons
⅔ cup	=	⅓ cup		1 teaspoon	=	½ teaspoon
½ cup	=	¼ cup		½ teaspoon	=	¼ teaspoon
⅓ cup	=	2 tablespoons + 2 teaspoons		¼ teaspoon	=	⅛ teaspoon

Now, I know what you're thinking: *"How the heck can I half a recipe when it calls for an uneven number of eggs?"* Don't fret—this is a totally doable task!

Here's what you have to do: Simply crack your egg into a bowl, whisk until completely blended, and then split it in half. To ensure you split the egg evenly, you can either measure or weigh it. First let's talk measurements. A large egg *(which is the size I use in all of my recipes)* measures close to ¼ cup. So, halving it would give you approximately two tablespoons. If you choose to check your accuracy by weight, you can simply measure your beaten egg and then divide. As a general rule of thumb, one large egg weighs about 1.75 ounces without the shell. So, half an egg will weigh close to one ounce. Technically it would be .875, but most digital scales don't get that granular.

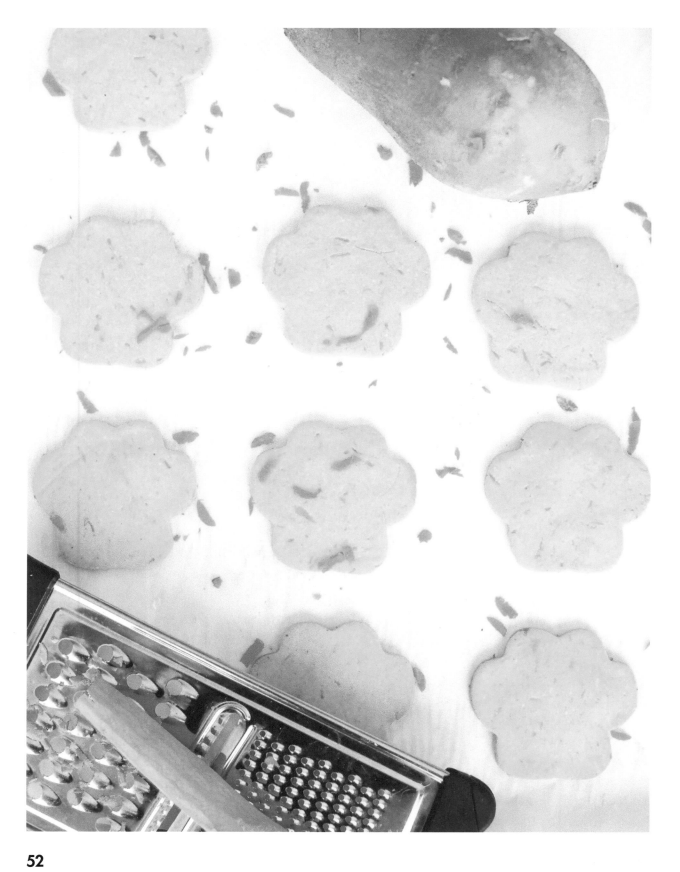

Sweet Potato Prints

Along with being tail-wagging good, sweet potatoes are super nutritious and healthy for our canines. Make sure it's fully cooled before adding it to your mixing bowl—*trust me, your hands will thank you for it once you start kneading!* Speaking of kneading your dough, you'll notice this is a slightly stickier mixture than some of the other recipes in this Gluten-Free Biscuits chapter. That's exactly why I emphasize letting your dough rest in the freezer for 15 minutes before rolling it out flat (just like you would a human cookie dough recipe). Even if you're in a pinch for time, don't skip this freezer step—it's essential for Sweet Potato Prints success!

INGREDIENTS:

1½ cups brown rice flour

1 cup almond flour

¼ cup coconut flour

½ teaspoon ground chia seeds

½ cup cooked, peeled, and mashed sweet potato

¼ cup peeled and finely grated carrot

2 tablespoons water

1 large egg

NOTES:

🐾 *When measuring your sweet potato, do not pack it down into the measuring cup. If you do, your dough will become too dense and sticky.

🐾 Store in airtight container in the refrigerator for up to five days or in the freezer up to one month.

DIRECTIONS:

1 Preheat oven to 350°F.

2 Line one baking sheet with parchment paper. Set aside.

3 In a large mixing bowl, add brown rice flour, almond flour, coconut flour, and ground chia seeds. Whisk together.

4 In a separate bowl, mash cooked sweet potato (no skin) and then measure out ½ cup*.

5 Add carrots, water, and egg to sweet potato and mix until thoroughly combined.

6 Make a well in the center of your dry ingredients and add wet ingredients. Mix with a spoon or fork.

7 With your hands, knead dough for several minutes, eventually forming a dough ball. Dough will feel slightly sticky.

8 Let dough rest for 15 minutes in the freezer before rolling flat.

9 Sandwich dough ball between two sheets of parchment paper and roll flat (about ¼" thick) with a rolling pin.

10 Using a cookie cutter, stamp out biscuits.

11 Place biscuits on baking sheet.

12 Bake 25–30 minutes.

13 Transfer biscuits to a wire rack to cool.

Garden Fresh Soft Chews

While treats certainly shouldn't replace your pup's daily meals, it's always great when you get to use treat-time as a way to sneak in some extra nutrient-dense veggies and fruits. Enter: Garden Fresh Soft Chews! They pack a nice serving of carrots and zucchini—both veggies provide immune-boosting vitamins. Plus, I've also included a banana and apple—both fruits offer digestive-aiding fiber. Another benefit? Unlike a traditional dog biscuit, these treats are designed to have a soft center, making them easy for both puppies and seniors to chew.

INGREDIENTS:

1 cup brown rice flour
½ cup peeled, finely grated, and packed carrots
½ cup peeled, finely grated, and packed zucchini
½ cup grated apple
1 mashed banana
1 egg
2 tablespoons coconut oil

NOTES:

 Avoid seeds when grating apple.
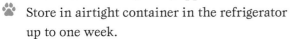 Store in airtight container in the refrigerator up to one week.

DIRECTIONS:

1   Preheat oven to 350°F.
2   Line a 9x13" baking sheet with parchment paper. Set aside.
3   In a large mixing bowl, add brown rice flour.
4   In a separate bowl, mix together grated carrots, grated zucchini, grated apple, mashed banana, egg, and coconut oil.
5   Add wet ingredients to flour and mix together with a fork or spoon until combined.
6   Spread your thick batter mixture onto the baking sheet, creating an even layer approximately ¼" thick.
7   Let mixture set for approximately 5 minutes.
8   Use a knife to score both horizontal and vertical lines, creating little squares.
9   Bake 40 minutes.
10 Remove from oven and carefully transfer to a wire rack to cool.
11 Once completely cooled, break or cut treats along the scored lines. You will be left with little square treats.

Banana Cinnamon Bursts

These bones are bursting with the three F's—fiber, fats, and flavor! After just a few minutes in the oven, a sweet smell will fill your kitchen. That's thanks to the almond flour, cinnamon, banana, and coconut oil. While these treats are sure to satisfy your pup's sweet tooth, there is absolutely no added sugar—just the natural sweetness from wholesome ingredients. Once the oven timer goes off, the edges of these treats should appear golden brown. While the center may still feel a bit cookie-like to touch *(be careful when you feel the treats, though, because they are extremely hot)*, they will harden as they cool.

INGREDIENTS:

2½ cups oat flour

1 cup almond flour

½ teaspoon cinnamon

1 mashed banana

2 tablespoons coconut oil

⅓ cup water

NOTES:

 Store in airtight container in the refrigerator up to three weeks or in the freezer up to three months.

DIRECTIONS:

1   Preheat oven to 350°F.

2   Line two baking sheets with parchment paper. Set aside.

3   In a large mixing bowl, add oat flour, almond flour, and cinnamon. Whisk together.

4   In a separate bowl, mash banana with a fork.

5   Add coconut oil and water to banana and mix together until thoroughly combined.

6   Make a well in the center of your dry ingredients and add wet ingredients. Mix together with a fork or spoon.

7   With your hands, knead dough for several minutes, eventually forming a dough ball. The dough will feel sticky.

8   Let dough ball rest on counter for about 5 minutes before rolling flat.

9   Sandwich dough ball between two sheets of parchment paper and roll flat (about ¼" thick) with a rolling pin.

10   Stamp with cookie cutters and place biscuits on baking sheet.

11   Bake for 20 minutes.

12   Transfer biscuits to a wire rack to cool.

Breakfast Bones

If you follow my blog—www.ProudDogMom.com— then you may recognize this Breakfast Bone recipe. It was actually the first homemade dog treat recipe I ever made. With only three ingredients, it doesn't get much simpler than this. I like to call this bone the Breakfast Bone because it's made with regular ol' instant oats, water, and an egg—the epitome of breakfast food. Of course, these bones should not replace your dog's breakfast meal and you don't only have to toss your pooch one of these biscuits in the a.m.!

INGREDIENTS:

3 cups instant oats
¾ cup water
1 large egg

NOTES:

- Bump up the nutritional value by adding ½ teaspoon of turmeric and a pinch of ground black pepper.
- Store in airtight container in the refrigerator up to three weeks or in the freezer up to three months.

DIRECTIONS:

1. Preheat oven to 350°F.
2. Line two baking sheets with parchment paper. Set aside.
3. Put all ingredients into a mixing bowl and mix together with a spoon or fork.
4. With your hands, knead dough for several minutes, eventually forming a dough ball. This dough will be a little sticky.
5. Let dough rest on the counter for about 15 minutes before rolling flat.
6. Sandwich dough ball between two sheets of parchment paper and roll flat (about ¼" thick) with a rolling pin.
7. Stamp with cookie cutters and place biscuits on baking sheet.
8. Bake for 30 minutes.
9. Transfer biscuits to a wire rack to cool.

The Skinny on Bouillon Cubes

Bouillon—a dehydrated stock that's formed into either granules or cubes—is a staple in many households because it's affordable, convenient, and loaded with flavor. Speaking of flavor, it comes in a variety of options, such as chicken, beef, and vegetable. Just add a little bouillon to your boiling water and voilà—you have yourself a quick and easy soup base. Along with seeing the popular ingredient in many human recipes, bouillon is commonly listed as an ingredient in homemade dog biscuits. But you may want to think twice before actually using it!

You see, some recipe writers use bouillon in their dog treat recipes in place of plain water as a way to create a richer treat taste that will make a dog's tail wag extra hard. The problem? Bouillon is typically processed with large amounts of sodium, sugar, MSG, and other additives. Plus, it often contains onion powder, garlic powder, and other ingredients your dog should avoid.

So, what should you do?

If you really want to make healthy dog treats and bump up the flavor with a yummy liquid, skip the bouillon and make your own stock instead. Simply boil skinless chicken or lean beef along with some dog-approved veggies (like carrots or celery), and you'll be left with a delicious and nutritious stock. Another benefit? You get to use the cooked meat and veggies too!

Apple Cinnamon Sticks

This recipe started out as a puppy-approved French toast stick and included a moderate amount of 100% pure maple syrup. Oh boy, did my dogs love it. But one day I decided to test out the recipe without the extra sugars. Sure, pure maple syrup is better for you and your pooch than refined sugar, but, at the end of the day, it's still sugar. And you know what happened? They still wagged their tails and gobbled it right down. Often times, we feel the need to add in overly sweet or flavorful ingredients to make the end result better suit our taste preferences—*because if we like it better than our dogs must too, right?!* The thing is, though, while humans have approximately 9,000 taste buds, canines only have around 1,700. Research shows that dogs can tell the difference between sweet, salty, sour, and bitter, but our fur kids certainly don't *need* maple syrup in their treats like we may crave.

INGREDIENTS:

1½ cups oat flour
1½ cups buckwheat flour
½ teaspoon cinnamon
½ cup all-natural applesauce
¼ cup water
1 large egg

NOTES:

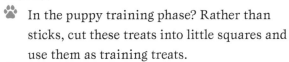 In the puppy training phase? Rather than sticks, cut these treats into little squares and use them as training treats.

Store in airtight container in the refrigerator for one-two weeks or in the freezer up to three months.

DIRECTIONS:

1 Preheat oven to 350°F.
2 In a large mixing bowl, add oat flour, buckwheat flour, and cinnamon. Whisk together.
3 In a separate bowl, mix applesauce, water, and egg.
4 Make a well in the center of your dry ingredients and add wet ingredients. Mix together with a fork or spoon.
5 With your hands, knead dough for several minutes, eventually forming a dough ball.
6 Sandwich dough ball between two sheets of parchment paper and roll flat (about ¼" thick) with a rolling pin. Roll into a rectangle.
7 Remove top parchment paper and set aside.
8 Grab the bottom piece of parchment paper with flatted dough on top and pull it onto a large baking sheet.
9 Using a knife, score dough into sticks.
10 Bake for 25–30 minutes.
11 Transfer biscuits to a wire rack to cool.

Peanut Butter Bones

If there's one food that makes dogs stand on their hind legs and jump up for joy, it's peanut butter. There's something about the creamy texture and rich flavor that dogs go nuts for. While a moderate amount of peanut butter is healthy for your pooch—since it contains protein and healthy fats—you must be extremely careful when selecting the perfect peanut butter to include in your homemade dog treats. Scan the ingredient label and make sure the naturally-derived sweetener Xylitol isn't listed. While this sugar alternative is commonly used in sugar-free foods and considered safe for humans, it's extremely toxic to dogs. Find out more about Xylitol on page 19 in The Dog Chef Pantry chapter.

INGREDIENTS:

3 cups brown rice flour

1 cup oat flour

¾ cup water

½ cup organic peanut butter

½ cup 100% pure pumpkin purée

NOTES:

 Store in airtight container in the refrigerator up to three weeks or in the freezer up to three months.

DIRECTIONS:

1   Preheat oven to 350°F.
2   Line two baking sheets with parchment paper. Set aside.
3   In a mixing bowl, add brown rice and oat flours. Whisk together.
4   Make a well in the center of your dry ingredients and add water, peanut butter, and pumpkin purée. Mix with a spoon or fork.
5   With your hands, knead dough for several minutes, eventually forming a dough ball.
6   Sandwich dough ball between two sheets of parchment paper and roll flat (about ¼" thick) with a rolling pin.
7   Using a cookie cutter, stamp out biscuits.
8   Place biscuits on baking sheet.
9   Bake for 25–30 minutes.
10 Transfer biscuits to a wire rack to cool.

Grain-Free Biscuits

The Recipes

Buckwheat Bones

Rich in various vitamins, protein, and fiber, buckwheat is a great grain-free flour that you can use to make homemade dog biscuits. While some call it a grain, it's actually made from fruit seeds that are closely related to rhubarb. Buckwheat flour offers a rather bold, nutty flavor that dogs love. In this recipe, I've paired buckwheat flour with almond flour, peanut butter, and mashed banana. Trust me—they come out as delicious as they sound. I would like to take a second and emphasize how yummy these bad boys smell. From the time you knead the biscuit dough to each time you open up your air-tight container filled with treats, they offer a strong nutty aroma. Get ready for some aggressive tail wagging!

INGREDIENTS:

1¼ cups buckwheat flour

¾ cup almond flour

1 mashed banana

2 tablespoons organic peanut butter

2 tablespoons water

NOTES:

 Store in airtight container on the counter for up to one week, in the refrigerator for up to three weeks, or in the freezer up to three months.

DIRECTIONS:

1 Preheat oven to 350°F.

2 Line one baking sheet with parchment paper. Set aside.

3 In a large mixing bowl, add buckwheat and almond flours. Whisk together.

4 In a separate bowl, mash banana with a fork.

5 Add peanut butter and water to banana and mix together until thoroughly combined.

6 Make a well in the center of your flours and add wet ingredients. Mix together with a spoon or fork.

7 With your hands, knead dough for several minutes, eventually forming a dough ball. When you're mixing this dough, it starts out feeling a bit powdery. Just keep kneading and folding onto itself until it takes on a Play Doh-like consistency.

8 Sandwich dough ball between two sheets of parchment paper and roll flat (about ¼" thick) with a rolling pin.

9 Stamp with cookie cutters and place biscuits on baking sheet.

10 Bake for 20 minutes.

11 Transfer biscuits to a wire rack to cool.

Nutty for Nut Bones

When it comes to homemade dog treats, I definitely have my favorites. From this chapter, I must admit, these are one of my top go-tos. The dough is easy to work with, the final product stores well, the treats are loaded with flavors that dogs love *(hello peanut butter)*, and they're nutrient rich. Let's chat about their goodness for a second! Both flours are naturally gluten-free and grain-free; ground flaxseeds are high in Omega-3 fatty acids; ground ginger has anti-inflammatory properties and aids digestion;

peanut butter is high in protein and healthy fats. Of course, each ingredient has a laundry list of benefits—these are just to name a few! When making these biscuits, be prepared for your hands to get a bit oily. That's because natural oils from the peanut butter and flaxseeds release as you knead the dough. So if you're looking for an all-natural hand moisturizer, I suppose all you need to do is whip up a batch of these!

INGREDIENTS:

2 cups super fine almond flour
½ cup coconut flour
2 tablespoons ground flaxseeds
1 teaspoon ground ginger
½ cup organic peanut butter
½ cup water

NOTES:

 Store in airtight container in the refrigerator up to three weeks or in the freezer up to three months.

DIRECTIONS:

1   Preheat oven to 350°F.
2   Line two baking sheets with parchment paper. Set aside.
3   In a large mixing bowl, add almond flour, coconut flour, ground flaxseeds, and ground ginger. Whisk together.
4   Make a well in the center of your dry ingredients and add peanut butter and water. Mix together with a fork or spoon.
5   With your hands, knead dough for several minutes, eventually forming a dough ball.
6   Sandwich dough ball between two sheets of parchment paper and roll flat (about ¼" thick) with a rolling pin.
7   Using a cookie cutter, stamp out biscuits.
8   Place biscuits on baking sheet.
9   Bake for 25–30 minutes.
10 Transfer biscuits to a wire rack to cool.

Banana Bread Soft Chews

Unlike the other biscuit recipes in this chapter, which create a crunchy snack, these soft chew dog treats are … well … soft on the inside. Once baked, they have more of a bread or cake-like texture. Since they don't require any real jaw power to chomp through, they're perfect for both baby and senior Fido … and every age in-between! Another benefit? Prep time is practically slashed in half because you don't have to whip out any cookie cutters and stand there stamping out shapes. Simply pour and spread your batter onto a baking sheet, score little squares, and pop them into the oven. It's that simple!

INGREDIENTS:

½ cup coconut flour

1 tablespoon ground flaxseed

½ cup 100% pure pumpkin purée

2 large eggs

1 mashed banana

1 tablespoon coconut oil

NOTES:

🐾 Store in airtight container in the refrigerator for one-two weeks.

DIRECTIONS:

1　Preheat oven to 350°F.

2　Line a 9x13" baking sheet with parchment paper. Set aside.

3　In a small mixing bowl, add coconut flour and ground flaxseeds. Whisk together.

4　In a separate bowl, mix together pumpkin purée, eggs, mashed banana, and coconut oil.

5　Add dry ingredients to the wet ingredients. Mix together with a spoon until thoroughly combined and consistency reaches a thick batter.

6　Spoon and spread your thick batter mixture onto the baking sheet, creating an even layer approximately ¼" thick.

7　Let mixture set for approximately 5 minutes.

8　Use a knife to score both horizontal and vertical lines, creating little squares.

9　Bake for 35 minutes.

10　Remove from oven and transfer to a wire rack to cool.

11　Once completely cooled, break or cut treats along the scored lines. You will be left with little square treats.

What's the Difference Between Gluten-Free and Grain-Free?

As more and more people are ditching gluten and grains when cooking their own meals, a lot are also switching their dogs to a gluten-free or completely grain-free diet. Despite the rise in popularity, there are still many who don't know what the two terms mean or how they differ. Keeping it very simple, let's take a quick look at these dietary choices.

What Is Gluten?

When most people think of gluten, they immediately think of bread, pizza, cereal, and other carbohydrate-heavy foods. However, gluten is actually the name for a protein that's found in certain grains, such as, wheat, rye, barley, and triticale—*which is a combination of wheat and rye.* Gluten, which is often referred to as a "sticky protein," functions like a glue and helps certain foods maintain their shape. If you follow a gluten-free diet then you must eliminate wheat, rye, barley, and triticale from your diet.

What Are Grains?

Wheat, rye, barley, triticale, oats, and rice are all considered grains. It's important to note that one can be gluten-free without being 100% grain-free, since not all grains contain gluten. However, when following a grain-free lifestyle, you will naturally eliminate all gluten-laden foods.

Grain-Free Dog Foods Don't Necessarily Mean Low-Carb

This is a huge misconception. If you switched your dog to a grain-free diet in hopes of reducing the number of carbohydrates your pooch eats in a day then you may be barking up the wrong tree. You see, carbs are necessary to form kibble. So many grain-free foods replace wheat and corn with options such as potatoes, sweet potatoes, and legumes. If you really want to cut carbohydrates out of your dog's diet, consider feeding fresh foods and homemade meals.

Should Your Dog Eat Gluten or Grain-Free?

This is one question that I can't really answer for you. While I personally feed my dogs a gluten-free diet, there are arguments for and against it. Obviously, if your dog suffers from any health issues that require a gluten-free and/or grain-free diet then definitely make the switch. But figuring out what you should feed your dog on a daily basis is a big decision. Only you, and perhaps your veterinarian, know what's best for your little fur baby.

Protein Power Bites

Protein is an essential part of a healthy and balanced canine diet. Just like with humans, protein provides your dog energy, helps build and repair their muscles, keeps their immune system strong, assists in forming new skin cells, and much more. While I personally feed my dogs a high-quality source of animal protein during meal time, I also love rewarding them with a protein-packed snack on occasion. These crunchy biscuits get their protein from quinoa flour and eggs. It's important to note that nutritional needs vary depending on a dog's age and activity level. So, check with your vet to see how much protein is recommended in your dog's diet.

INGREDIENTS:

1½ cups quinoa flour

½ cup coconut flour

¼ teaspoon turmeric

Pinch ground black pepper

1 egg

¼ cup all-natural applesauce

2 tablespoons water

2 teaspoons coconut oil

NOTES:

 Store in airtight container in the refrigerator up to two weeks or in the freezer up to three months.

DIRECTIONS:

1   Preheat oven to 325°F.

2   Line one baking sheet with parchment paper. Set aside.

3   In a large mixing bowl, add quinoa flour, coconut flour, turmeric, and black pepper. Whisk to combine.

4   In a separate bowl, whisk egg.

5   Add applesauce, water, and coconut oil to egg. Mix together until combined.

6   Add wet ingredients to dry ingredients and mix together with a spoon or fork.

7   Using your hands, knead dough for several minutes, eventually forming a dough ball. Dough will feel dry at first, just keep folding and kneading.

8   Sandwich dough between two layers of parchment paper.

9   With a rolling pin, carefully roll dough to about ¼" thick.

10   Stamp with cookie cutters and place biscuits on baking sheet.

11   Bake for 25 minutes.

12   After the timer goes off, remove biscuits from oven, flip them over, and bake for another 5 minutes.

13   Transfer biscuits to a wire rack to cool.

Peanut Butter Doggy Donuts & Holes

This recipe is so much fun because you really get two treats out of one dough—the doggy donuts and the donut holes! They aren't cakey like a human donut. Rather, they are shaped like donuts and have the texture of a crunchy dog biscuit. Catering to the canine taste preference, these treats have a strong flavor of peanut butter and banana. Because, seriously, what dog doesn't love peanut butter and banana?! In this recipe, I pair the bark-worthy ingredients with garbanzo bean flour, which is a wholesome, grain-free flour made from ground-up chickpeas. Along with its creamy texture and naturally sweet flavor, garbanzo bean flour is high in fiber and protein. So, these doggy donuts are actually healthy. Just make sure to read the directions and notes carefully before whipping up a batch because they can burn pretty easily.

INGREDIENTS:

2¼ cups garbanzo bean flour

1 large egg

1 mashed banana

¼ cup organic peanut butter

NOTES:

- These treats can burn easily. Make sure to flip them over after 12–15 minutes in the oven, or when the bottoms turn golden brown.
- I typically bake the donuts on one tray and the holes on another. Since the holes are smaller, they need less time to bake.
- Peanut butter icing recipe featured in photo on page 158.
- Store non-iced treats in airtight container in the refrigerator up to two weeks or in the freezer up to three months.

DIRECTIONS:

1 Preheat oven to 350°F.
2 Line two baking sheets with parchment paper. Set aside.
3 In a large mixing bowl, add garbanzo bean flour and whisk to eliminate lumps.
4 In a separate mixing bowl, whisk egg.
5 Add well-mashed banana and room temperature peanut butter to egg. Mix until thoroughly combined.
6 Make a well in the center of your flour and add wet ingredients. Mix with a spoon or fork.
7 With your hands, knead dough for several minutes, eventually forming a dough ball.
8 Let rest in freezer for 15 minutes.
9 Sandwich dough ball between two sheets of parchment paper and roll flat (about ¼" thick) with a rolling pin.
10 Using one large circle cookie cutter and one small circle cookie cutter, stamp out donut shapes.
11 Place donuts and holes on a parchment paper-lined baking sheet and bake for 12–15 minutes.
12 After the timer goes off, remove donuts and holes from oven, flip them over, and bake for another 5 minutes.
13 Transfer to a wire rack to cool.

What's the Deal with Baby Food?

*H*ave you ever come across a homemade dog treat recipe that calls for baby food? Chances are, if you've glanced through Pinterest or done a simple Google search then the answer is yes. While baby food itself isn't toxic to dogs, you may notice that I don't use it in my recipes. There are a couple of reasons for this:

1 *Some Baby Food Jars Contain Spices That Are Toxic to Dogs.* It's not uncommon to find onion, onion juice, or onion powder listed as an ingredient in baby food. It's the same with garlic. While those additions are perfectly fine for two-legged human babies, they're toxic to your four-legged fur babies.

2 *Most Baby Food Jars Contain Unnecessary Extras.* It's also not uncommon to find extra flavorings, extracts, concentrates, and preservatives in those little baby food jars. I recently looked at the ingredient list for a jar of banana baby food and noticed, along with ripened bananas, it included concentrates, citric acid, and ascorbic acid. Although there isn't anything harmful on that list, when cooking for Fido, I like to keep things as natural as possible.

So why not just make your own?

You can easily replicate any baby food flavor right in your own home, using fresh ingredients. If you need puréed bananas then just bust out your blender and purée them yourself. If you need some puréed chicken for a recipe then just pop a boneless chicken breast *(all skin and fat removed)* into a pot of water, boil until fully cooked, purée in a blender, and voilà. You can have whatever you need in no time. Plus, it will be 100% fresh, natural, and preservative-free!

Sweet Treat Biscuits

As my love affair with garbanzo bean flour continued to flourish, I came up with these delicious and nutritious biscuits. They're loaded with all the healthful goodness and natural sweetness that apples and carrots provide. When making these biscuits, it's important to note that the dough will seem dry and crumbly at first. While you may be compelled to add a spoon or so of liquid to your dough, just keep folding and kneading. Trust me—too much liquid in this recipe makes the dough very sticky and difficult to work with. So stay with the listed measurements. After several minutes, the dough will become smooth and moldable—it's a texture that's easy to roll out and stamp with cookie cutters. Plus, once the treats are baked, I bet they'll make your pup's tail wag!

INGREDIENTS:
2 cups garbanzo bean flour
½ cup coconut flour
½ cup all-natural applesauce
½ cup peeled and finely grated carrots
1 tablespoon coconut oil

NOTES:
- When measuring carrots, don't pack them down. If you do, your mixture will come out too wet and a bit sticky.
- When you first begin kneading this dough, it will seem a bit dry and crumbly. Just keep folding and kneading until all of the ingredients come together—this will take several minutes.
- This recipe is also great with a few chopped mint leaves added to the dough!
- Store in airtight container in the refrigerator up to two weeks or in the freezer up to three months.

DIRECTIONS:
1 Preheat oven to 325°F.
2 Line two baking sheets with parchment paper. Set aside.
3 In a large mixing bowl, add garbanzo bean and coconut flours. Whisk together.
4 In a separate bowl, mix together applesauce, grated carrots, and coconut oil.
5 Make a well in the center of your dry ingredients and add wet ingredients. Mix together with a fork or spoon.
6 With your hands, knead dough for several minutes, eventually forming a dough ball.
7 Sandwich dough ball between two sheets of parchment paper and roll flat (about ¼" thick) with a rolling pin.
8 Using a cookie cutter, stamp out biscuits.
9 Place biscuits on baking sheet.
10 Bake 25–30 minutes.
11 After the timer goes off, remove biscuits from oven, flip them over, and bake for another 5 minutes.
12 Transfer biscuits to a wire rack to cool.

Chickpea Cookie Biscuits

These treats are sort of like a cross between a biscuit and a cookie—the outside is hard and crunchy like a biscuit while the inside is a bit softer like a cookie. That's thanks to the blend of garbanzo bean and coconut flours. While it took me a few attempts to get this recipe just right, I knew by the third try adjusting measurements and swapping ingredients that it was a keeper. A quick heads up: When making these treats, your dough ball will become a bit dense. So get your muscles ready because it's definitely worth the little arm workout you get when rolling out the dough. Since this dough is a bit stiffer, I like to flatten it out with my fingers before busting out the rolling pin. But once you work with it, you'll figure out what works best for you.

INGREDIENTS:

2½ cups garbanzo bean flour
½ cup coconut flour
2 tablespoons ground flaxseeds
½ cup 100% pure pumpkin purée
1 large egg
3 tablespoons water

NOTES:

 Store in airtight container in the refrigerator up to two weeks or in the freezer up to three months.

DIRECTIONS:

1 Preheat oven to 350°F.
2 Line two baking sheets with parchment paper. Set aside.
3 In a large mixing bowl, add garbanzo bean flour, coconut flour, and ground flaxseeds. Whisk together.
4 Make a well in the center of your dry ingredients and add pumpkin purée, egg, and water. Mix with a spoon or fork.
5 With your hands, knead dough for several minutes, eventually forming a dough ball.
6 Sandwich dough ball between two sheets of parchment paper and roll flat (about ¼" thick) with a rolling pin.
7 Using a cookie cutter, stamp out biscuits.
8 Place biscuits on baking sheet.
9 Bake 25 minutes.
10 Transfer biscuits to a wire rack to cool.

Green Veggie Superfood Bones

Looking for a creative way to add more veggies to your dog's diet? Try these superfood-packed green veggie bones. I used finely chopped kale and little broccoli floret bits to make these nourishing biscuits. As you look down the ingredient list, you'll notice I pack a lot of veggies into these bones. While you certainly can finely chop your greens with a knife, since there are a lot in here, I prefer to throw them into a food processor and pulse a few times before adding them to my dough. This makes my green bits super teeny tiny. If your veggies are too big, you may struggle to stamp out your biscuits because the veggies will get in the way. Although, if your biscuit shapes get a bit messy, I promise your dog won't mind!

INGREDIENTS:

2 cups super fine almond flour
½ cup coconut flour
1 fresh kale leaf
3 broccoli florets
½ cup water
2 tablespoons coconut oil

NOTES:

- Be careful not to over-process the veggies. You don't want to purée them.
- This dough is very fragile. Be careful when stamping out your biscuits.
- Since this dough is fragile, I prefer to use a small cookie cutter.
- Store in airtight container in the refrigerator up to five days or in the freezer up to one month.

DIRECTIONS:

1 Preheat oven to 350°F.
2 Line two baking sheets with parchment paper. Set aside.
3 In a large mixing bowl, add almond and coconut flours. Set aside.
4 Put kale leaf (not the spine) and broccoli florets into a food processor and pulse until finely chopped. Do not over-process—you don't want mushy veggies.
5 Add chopped veggies into mixing bowl and whisk together.
6 Make a well in the center of your dry ingredients and add water and coconut oil. Mix with a spoon or fork.
7 With your hands, knead dough for several minutes, eventually forming a dough ball.
8 Let dough rest in freezer for 15 minutes.
9 Sandwich dough ball between two sheets of parchment paper and roll flat (about ¼" thick) with a rolling pin.
10 Using a cookie cutter, stamp out biscuits.
11 Place biscuits on baking sheet.
12 Bake 25 minutes, or until edges are golden.
13 Transfer biscuits to a wire rack to cool.

Burgers & Bites

The Recipes

Puppy Veggie Frittatas

On weekends, I like to go all out for breakfast. For the humans, I typically whip up eggs, French toast, hash browns, bacon, sausage, and mimosas. *So delicious.* For the dogs, I make them their own plate of scrambled eggs. They go nuts for eggs. In an attempt to squeeze more veggies into their diet, I decided to bump their breakfast up a notch and created these Puppy Veggie Frittatas. Since I had spinach in the fridge the first time I made this recipe, I created spinach frittatas. But you can really use any dog-approved veggie. Try it out with chopped kale, shredded zucchini, shredded carrots, or little broccoli bits. These frittatas are a hit with my dogs, and they've become a weekend brunch staple in my household.

INGREDIENTS:

2 large eggs

¼ teaspoon turmeric

Pinch ground black pepper

1 packed cup of spinach, finely chopped

Coconut oil, to coat pan

NOTES:

- Do not under-bake or your frittatas will be runny.
- Do not serve straight from the oven so they don't burn your dog's mouth. Let them cool.
- Store in airtight container in the refrigerator up to three days.

DIRECTIONS:

1   Preheat oven to 400°F.
2   In a small mixing bowl, crack two eggs and whisk together.
3   Add turmeric and ground black pepper to eggs. Mix and set aside.
4   Measure one cup packed spinach.
5   Remove stems and finely chop spinach.
6   Add spinach to eggs and mix well.
7   Grease silicone mold tray with coconut oil.
8   Fill each mold in silicone tray ¾ way up. The eggs will puff when baking.
9   Bake in oven for approximately 20 minutes. Stick a toothpick into the center of each frittata to check doneness. Toothpick will come out clean when done.
10 Remove from oven, let cool, then remove frittatas from mold.

Salmon Burgers

The first time I made these mini salmon burgers for my dogs, I loved them so much that I decided to bake a second batch for myself! The best part? They only take 20 minutes to make from start to finish. For convenience, I use wild caught canned salmon versus a fresh salmon fillet. Yes, canned salmon is safe for your dogs to eat. In fact, it's insanely healthy since it's rich in Omega-3 fatty acids, healthy fats, and protein. If you're someone who eats a lot of salmon, I don't recommend using up your leftovers to create these puppy burgers because it may have some not-good-for-your-dog spices sprinkled on it.

INGREDIENTS:

1 can wild caught salmon, in water (5 oz)
1 large egg
½ cup super fine almond flour

NOTES:

- Do not under-bake.
- I like to use extra virgin olive oil to grease my muffin tin. Use whatever healthy oil you have on hand!
- Do not serve straight from the oven so they don't burn your dog's mouth. Let them cool.
- Store in airtight container in the refrigerator up to three days.

DIRECTIONS:

1 Preheat oven to 350°F.
2 Drain canned salmon.
3 In a small mixing bowl, mash salmon with a fork to ensure there aren't any chunks.
4 Add egg and almond flour to salmon. Mix together with a spoon or fork until thoroughly combined.
5 Use a greased muffin tin—or mini muffin tin if you have small dogs—to help shape the salmon burgers. Simply add a spoon of the salmon mixture into each muffin hole. Make each salmon burger approximately ¼" thick.
6 Bake for 15 minutes, or until set.
7 Transfer to a wire rack to cool.

93

Bone Burgers (3 Ways)

These little bone burgers take about 20 minutes to make from start to finish and are bound to please your pup's taste buds. When shopping for chopped meat, look for the lowest fat option—I use 95% lean. I also recommend making small batches of these bone burgers since their shelf life isn't that long (only up to three days in the fridge). That's why you'll notice I only use a ¼ pound of beef in each version. Which brings me to my next note: There are many ways you can make these bones. I've outlined three versions to get you started, but feel free to play around with adding other dog-approved veggies, herbs, and spices. The first version I've included in this book is a plain bone burger—the only ingredient is a ¼ pound extra lean chopped meat. In the second version—a cheese bone burger—I've add shredded cheddar cheese to the beef. Lastly, in the third version, I boost Omega-3s and fiber by adding a spoonful of ground flaxseeds!

INGREDIENTS:

¼ pound extra lean ground beef (needed for each version)
VERSION 2: ¼ cup shredded cheddar cheese
VERSION 3: 1 teaspoon ground flaxseeds

NOTES:

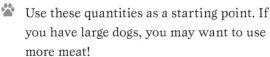 Use these quantities as a starting point. If you have large dogs, you may want to use more meat!

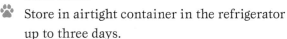 Store in airtight container in the refrigerator up to three days.

DIRECTIONS:

1 Preheat oven to 350°F.

2 If making bone burgers version 1 just skip to #3. If making version 2 or 3, combine ground beef with cheese or flaxseeds.

3 Pack ground beef into silicone bone mold. No need to grease the mold since the beef's fat will release when cooking and naturally lubricate the mold.

4 Bake for 15 minutes.

5 Transfer to a wire rack to cool.

Chicken & Carrot Quiche Paws

Protein is the star of the show here. These chicken and carrot quiche paws are simply boiled and puréed chicken mixed with puréed carrot and an egg. That's it! Once baked, these quiche paws remain soft and easy to chew, making them perfect for a senior pooch.

While I call these little chicken morsels a healthy *treat*, depending on the size of your silicone mold, they can be a rather filling snack. Make sure to work these around your dog's regular meals and pay attention to portion sizes.

INGREDIENTS:

4 cups water (to boil chicken)
1 boneless chicken breast (8 ounces)
1 large carrot, peeled and chopped
1 large egg
Olive oil, to grease mold

NOTES:

- Trim all visible fat before cooking chicken breast.
- Store in airtight container in the refrigerator up to three days or in freezer up to one month.

DIRECTIONS:

1 Preheat oven to 350°F.
2 Fill a saucepan with water and boil chicken until fully cooked.
3 Let chicken cool.
4 With a fork, shred chicken.
5 Purée chicken in a blender with chopped carrot.
6 In a mixing bowl, whisk egg.
7 Add puréed chicken and carrot mixture to egg and thoroughly combine.
8 Lightly grease silicone mold with olive oil.
9 Spoon mixture into mold and pat down firmly.
10 Bake for 25 minutes.
11 Let cool for 10–15 minutes in molds.
12 Transfer to a wire rack to continue cooling.

Chicken Quiche with a Kick

This recipe is very similar to the Chicken & Carrot Quiche Paws on the last page, but I've included a few extra ingredients to bump up the nutritional value. I swapped out the carrot with some pumpkin purée, which adds a nice dose of fiber to these treats. Did you know fiber is great for your dog's digestive health? Plus, I've included a small spoonful of turmeric. Find out why I'm so obsessed with turmeric and why I pair it with a pinch of black pepper on page 101. Aside from the many health benefits, these Chicken Quiche with a Kick treats are also incredibly delicious and satisfying. I promise your dog will want to thank you for them!

INGREDIENTS:

4 cups water (to boil chicken)

1 boneless chicken breast (8 ounces)

½ cup 100% pure pumpkin purée

1 large egg

½ teaspoon turmeric

Pinch of ground black pepper

Olive oil, to grease mold

NOTES:

🐾 Trim all visible fat before cooking chicken breast.

🐾 Store in airtight container in the refrigerator up to three days or in freezer up to one month.

DIRECTIONS:

1   Preheat oven to 350°F.

2   Fill saucepan with water.

3   Add chicken breast and boil until fully cooked.

4   Let cool.

5   With a fork, shred chicken.

6   Purée chicken in a blender.

7   In a mixing bowl, thoroughly combine puréed chicken, pumpkin purée, egg, turmeric, and ground black pepper.

8   Lightly grease silicone mold with olive oil.

9   Spoon mixture into mold and pat down firmly.

10   Bake for 25 minutes.

11   Let cool for 10–15 minutes in molds.

12   Transfer to a wire rack to continue cooling.

Let's Talk Turmeric

As you flip through the recipes in this book, you'll notice turmeric sprinkled in many of my recipes. I use it quite often because it's just so darn good for our dogs. In fact, you can usually tell that I've been cooking for my dogs just by glancing down at my yellow-stained fingertips.

You see, turmeric is a yellow spice that's commonly used to flavor Indian cuisine. Along with its blasts of flavor, the powerful spice has been used for its medicinal purposes for centuries.

Turmeric's therapeutic benefits are believed to be a result of the bioactive ingredient curcumin *(not to be confused with cumin)*. Along with being a super-spice for us humans, pet nutritionists also recommend giving it to canines. Similar to how turmeric benefits humans, adding it to your dog's diet is believed to help ward off cancer, fight inflammation, ease arthritis symptoms, aid digestion, and much more.

When it comes to adding turmeric to your dog's diet, there are a few things you need to know. First of all, it's hard for a dog's body to absorb the curcumin in turmeric when given by itself. That's why experts recommend combining it with a healthy fat, like coconut oil. You can also drastically increase the absorbency by pairing the spice with some ground black pepper.

It's important to remember that a little turmeric goes a long way. Start with about ¼ teaspoon per day for small dogs, and up to a teaspoon per day for large dogs. As with any ingredient, add it to your dog's diet slowly to ensure your dog is digesting it well. If your dog suffers from any medical conditions or is on any medications, consult with your veterinarian before adding turmeric to his/her diet.

Jerky, Chews & Chips

The Recipes

Chicken Jerky

If you're looking for a chicken jerky recipe that's easy, healthy, and one your fur baby will love then you need to try this one. I started making this home-made chicken jerky a few years ago after I looked through the ingredient label of my former favorite store-bought treats. While they were advertised as "All-Natural," one of the first ingredients listed on the bag was sugar … followed by a whole bunch of preservatives and ingredients I couldn't pronounce. Since I'm careful with what I feed my dogs, I imme-diately boycotted commercial jerky and decided I was much better off making my own. The best part about this recipe is it only has one ingredient. That's right—just one. CHICKEN! There are no preserva-tives added. No sugar. No salt. Nothing extra. Just chicken. When I gave my chicken jerky to my dogs for the first time, they gobbled it right up. I mean, what's not to love? From your dog's point of view, they're getting a delicious treat. From my point of view, they're eating a healthy, high-protein snack. That's not to mention how easy they are to make!

INGREDIENTS:

1 pound boneless chicken breast
Olive oil, to grease wire rack

NOTES:
- Cook time will vary depending on how thick or thin you slice your chicken.
- If chicken strips get stuck to the wire rack then use a spatula to help release.
- Since there are no preservatives added to this jerky to extend the shelf life, I only like to keep them for up to two weeks in an airtight container. While you don't have to refrigerate them (because they're fully dried out), I personally still like to.

DIRECTIONS:
1 Preheat oven to 250°F.
2 Trim the chicken of all visible fat.
3 Rinse and pat dry. Set aside.
4 Line a baking sheet with parchment paper.
5 Place a wire rack onto the cookie sheet—this will allow the air to circulate as the chicken is dehydrating—and lightly grease with olive oil.
6 Slice the chicken ⅛" to ¼" thick.
7 Place the chicken slices on a rack and cook for 2 hours.
8 After 2 hours, remove from oven, flip chicken strips over, and continue cooking for another 45 minutes (or until it's all dried out). *Since everyone's oven can vary, check jerky every 30 minutes or so to ensure it doesn't burn.*

Beef Jerky

Dogs love jerky so why stop at just chicken? This homemade beef jerky is simple to make—just slice a lean cut of beef into thin strips and dehydrate it in the oven until it's completely dried out. Let's talk beef for a second. While you might love a marbled steak for your dinner, when picking the perfect cut of beef for your pooch's jerky meat the goal is to go as lean as possible. Aside from health reasons, fat will turn rancid very quickly, significantly decreasing the shelf life of your jerky. Ask your local butcher for cuts such as: eye of the round, bottom round, top round, sirloin, or flank.

INGREDIENTS:
1 pound lean beef
Olive oil, to grease wire rack

NOTES:
- Cook time will vary depending on how thick or thin you slice your beef.
- Store in the refrigerator in an airtight container up to one week.

DIRECTIONS:
1. Preheat oven to 250°F.
2. Line a baking sheet with parchment paper.
3. Place a wire rack onto the cookie sheet—this will allow the air to circulate as the beef is dehydrating—and lightly grease with olive oil.
4. Slice beef into ⅛" to ¼" thick strips.
5. Place the beef slices on a rack and cook for 2 hours.
6. After 2 hours, remove from oven, flip beef strips over, lower oven temperature to 200°, and continue cooking for another 1½ hours. *Since everyone's oven can vary, check jerky every 30 minutes or so to ensure it doesn't burn.*

Salmon Jerky

Sure, there are plenty of fish in the sea. But if your dog could only have one then salmon is a great choice! First of all, salmon is rich in Omega-3 fatty acids, which have been linked to decreased inflammation and improved heart health. It's also an excellent source of protein, potassium, and B vitamins. Another benefit of this salmon jerky recipe compared to my chicken and beef jerky recipes is that senior dogs who are dealing with dental issues may have an easier time eating it. That's because the salmon jerky remains relatively tender. *P.S. If you share this salmon jerky with your dog (which you should because it's delicious) then you may enjoy your human helping dipped in a little Sriracha Mayo sauce … yummmmm!*

INGREDIENTS:

½ pound fresh wild caught salmon

NOTES:

- If you don't have a filleting knife, use one with a long, thin, sharp blade. Don't use a serrated knife to fillet a fish.
- You can use either clean needle-nose pliers or a pair of tweezers to de-bone the fresh salmon.
- I find the salmon strips stick to the wire rack too easily, even when greased. So unlike my chicken and beef jerky recipes, I just dehydrate these on a piece of parchment paper. Since they aren't on a wire rack airing out, the cook time is longer.
- Cook time will vary depending on how thick or thin you slice your salmon.
- Store in the refrigerator in an airtight container up to five days.

DIRECTIONS:

1. Preheat oven to 200°F.
2. Line a baking sheet with parchment paper.
3. Fillet and de-bone fresh salmon fillet.
4. Slice salmon ⅛" to ¼" thick.
5. Place the salmon slices on parchment paper-lined baking sheet and cook for 3 hours.
6. Remove from oven, flip salmon strips over, and continue dehydrating for another 3 hours. *Since everyone is going to slice their fish a slightly different thickness, your jerky may be done sooner or require more time in the oven. Once you flip the strips over, check them every 30 minutes for desired doneness.*

Pumpkin Bark

Are you ready for a delicious-smelling kitchen? As this pumpkin bark dehydrates in the oven, a rather cozy aroma will fill your home. I made this recipe one day when I was in experiment mode. I wanted to find out what would happen if I mixed pumpkin purée with a few dog-approved spices, spread the mixture on a baking sheet, and let it dry out in the oven. The result? A fun pumpkin bark that will make your pooch, well, bark for a bite! The thinner you spread your mixture, the quicker it will dry out and become a crunchy texture. While I emphasize spreading an even layer of pumpkin before baking, chances are you'll have some thinner/thicker spots. If you remove the entire tray from the oven at the same time and are left with a few wetter pieces, no big deal! They aren't sticky at all—just softer *(which, if you have a senior dog, may even be a better consistency for your pup)*! The best part about making these at home is you get to play around and find what works best for you.

INGREDIENTS:

1 can (15 oz) 100% pure pumpkin purée
¼ teaspoon ground ginger
¼ teaspoon ground cinnamon

NOTES:

 Store in the refrigerator in an airtight container up to three days.

DIRECTIONS:

1　Preheat oven to 250°F.
2　Line a 9x13" baking sheet with parchment paper. Set aside.
3　In a mixing bowl, thoroughly combine all ingredients.
4　Thinly and evenly spread mixture onto parchment paper-lined baking sheet.
5　Bake for 3–3½ hours, depending on thickness and desired texture. Since everyone's bark may vary in thickness, make sure to check on it every 30 minutes. While the bark's edges will turn golden, you don't want it to burn.
6　Remove from oven.
7　Cut or rip dehydrated pumpkin mixture into little 1" pieces of "bark"
8　Let cool on a wire rack.

Sweet Potato Chips

I went through a lot of sweet potatoes when I was trying to perfect this recipe. At first, I tried setting my oven to a very low temperature and dehydrating the potatoes for a rather lengthy time. Then, I experimented with a higher heat for a short amount of time. Well, just like baby bear's porridge, I found a consistently crispy chip comes from something in the middle of my first two attempts! But there's a secret to creating the best sweet potato chips ever—soaking them in water for a few minutes before popping them in the oven. This helps to remove some of the starch from the potato, allowing the chips to crisp better as they're dehydrating in the oven. I can't stress enough the importance of the soaking step, so don't skip it just to save a few extra minutes. You'll be happy you took the time once you're pulling your tray of crispy, bright-orange chips out of the oven.

INGREDIENTS:

1 large sweet potato
1 bowl of cold water

NOTES:

- These chips can burn easily so keep a close eye on them. Some will be done quicker than others.
- Store at room temperature in an airtight container for up to five days.

DIRECTIONS:

1 Preheat oven to 300°F.
2 Line two baking sheets with parchment paper. Set aside.
3 Peel sweet potato.
4 Using a mandolin, thinly slice sweet potato (I cut mine about ⅛" thick).
5 Soak sweet potato rounds in a bowl of cold water for 10 minutes.
6 Pat soaked potato rounds dry with a paper towel.
7 Dehydrate in the oven for 30–40 minutes. Since the thickness and size of your chips will vary depending on the area of the potato they were cut from (skinny end or fat middle), some chips will take longer to crisp than others. While dehydrating, check sweet potatoes every 10 minutes until they all reach your desired doneness.
8 Remove from oven and transfer to a wire rack to cool.

Apple Chips

Dogs are known to have a sweet tooth and these apple chips are sure to satisfy. As the apples dehydrate in the oven, their natural sugars intensify, making them one heck of a good tasting treat! When making my apple chips, sometimes I leave the skin on and other times I peel them first. Since I slice my apples incredibly thin and the skin gets crunchy too, my dogs have always gobbled these down with ease. Plus, there are benefits to leaving the skin on since it contains fiber and a great deal of vitamins. Whip up a batch and enjoy listening to the loud crunch as your pooch bites down.

INGREDIENTS:

1 large apple

NOTES:

 Store at room temperature in an airtight container up to five days.

DIRECTIONS:

1 Preheat oven to 200°F.
2 Line two baking sheets with parchment paper. Set aside.
3 Core apple to remove all seeds.
4 Using a mandolin, thinly slice apple (I cut mine about ⅛" thick).
5 Place apple rounds on baking sheet in one layer. Make sure they do not overlap.
6 Dehydrate in the oven for 2 hours.
7 Flip and dehydrate apples for another 1 hour.
8 Turn off oven and let apples cool inside for 1 more hour. This will help them to crunch up.

Zucchini Chips

Crunchy, tasty, and downright addictive—those are the first few words that come to my mind when describing these zucchini chips. I was so excited the first time I made a batch of these healthy chips and my dogs gobbled them right down. They're low calorie and loaded with beneficial nutrients, making them perfect for the pooch who needs to watch his weight. Plus, did I mention how easy they are to make? Seriously, all you have to do is slice a zucchini into little rounds, brush a little bit of olive oil on top, and let them dehydrate in the oven. It doesn't get any easier than this!

INGREDIENTS:
1 large zucchini
Extra virgin olive oil

NOTES:
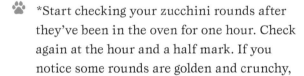 *Start checking your zucchini rounds after they've been in the oven for one hour. Check again at the hour and a half mark. If you notice some rounds are golden and crunchy, remove from oven before the two hours is up.

Store in the refrigerator in an airtight container up to one week.

DIRECTIONS:
1 Preheat oven to 225°F.
2 Line two baking sheets with parchment paper. Set aside.
3 Using a mandolin, thinly slice zucchini into rounds.
4 Sandwich zucchini rounds between paper towels to pull out some of the water content.
5 Place zucchini rounds on baking sheet. Make sure they do not overlap.
6 In a small bowl, pour a little olive oil.
7 Using a pastry brush, gently brush olive oil onto top of zucchini rounds. This olive oil coating should be very light!
8 Dehydrate in the oven for 2 hours, or until zucchini rounds become golden and crispy.*
9 Remove from oven and transfer to a wire rack to cool. They won't take long to cool.

Kale Chips

This is a healthy snack that both you and your pooch can enjoy together. And, oh boy, are they addicting! These superfood chips are light, crunchy, and bursting with flavor. They taste great plain with just a little oil, but if you want to bump up the nutritional value even more then you can always sprinkle a little ginger or turmeric on the kale leaves before popping them in the oven. Just remember—a little goes a long way when it comes to spices. As soon as you pull the tray of "chips" out of the oven, they'll be ready to go—no need to let them cool on a wire rack. I get such a kick out of listening to my little pups chomp away on these kale chips, and since they're super nutritious, I'm pretty generous with how many I let them eat. A serving of four or five kale chips makes for one happy canine.

INGREDIENTS:

1 bunch of kale

1 tablespoon coconut oil, melted down to liquid state

NOTES:

- 🐾 *Melt coconut oil in either a double boiler or the microwave for quick convenience.
- 🐾 If you don't have coconut oil, you can use extra virgin olive oil instead.
- 🐾 Store in the refrigerator in an airtight container up to one week.

DIRECTIONS:

1 Preheat oven to 275°F.

2 Wash and dry kale leaves.

3 Tear kale leaves off of the thick ribs, making your "chips" about 1–2" wide. Throw ribs away.

4 Put leaves into a large mixing bowl and coat with *liquid coconut oil.

5 Using your hands, massage the oil onto the leaves, ensuring they are evenly coated.

6 Spread kale leaves in a single layer on a baking sheet (you may need two or three baking sheets depending on how big your kale bunch is). The leaves shouldn't touch each other.

7 Bake in oven for 20 minutes, or until crispy.

8 Remove from oven and serve.

Quinoa Crisps

Quinoa is a powerhouse seed that's packed with protein, fiber, healthy fats, calcium, and other nutrients. While it's common for us humans to enjoy a fresh quinoa salad or spoon some onto the side of our dinner dish, did you know it's also a healthy food for dogs? Just make sure to only feed your canine companion rinsed and cooked quinoa. That's because the quinoa plant produces something called saponin to protect itself from insects, and saponin can cause an upset tummy. Simply washing and cooking the quinoa, though, will remove most of the saponin. In this recipe, I boiled the quinoa, mixed it with a few other wholesome ingredients, and baked it to form crackers. Enjoy!

INGREDIENTS:

¼ cup dry quinoa

½ cup water (to cook quinoa)

2 tablespoons cold water (to add after quinoa is cooked)

¼ cup garbanzo bean flour

¼ teaspoon turmeric

Pinch ground black pepper

NOTES:

 Store at room temperature in an airtight container up to five days.

DIRECTIONS:

1 Preheat oven to 350°F.

2 Rinse quinoa in a strainer.

3 Add quinoa and water into a small pot. Bring to a boil.

4 Once water starts boiling, cover the pot and turn stove down to low. Cook for about 12–15 minutes, or until quinoa has absorbed all of the water and is tender.

5 Transfer cooked quinoa to a mixing bowl. Add remaining water, garbanzo bean flour, turmeric, and black pepper.

6 Mix together until thoroughly combined. Set aside.

7 Line a baking sheet with parchment paper.

8 Using a 1 teaspoon measuring spoon, scoop quinoa mixture onto the baking sheet, and spread into a thin layer to create crackers.

9 Bake quinoa crackers for 15 minutes.

10 Using a spatula, turn crackers over and bake on the other side for another 15 minutes.

11 Remove from oven and transfer to a wire rack to cool.

Pupsicles

The Recipes

3-Ingredient Frosty Bones

With only three ingredients—coconut oil, a mashed banana, and ground ginger—you likely already have everything you need to whip up these frosty bones. Another benefit? They're super simple to make. The creamy treats take just minutes to prepare before tossing them in the freezer and, once most coconut oil-based treats hit the cold temperature, they don't take that long to set. So, let's talk portion control for a second. While coconut oil offers a lot of amazing health benefits, you don't want to overdo it. As a general rule of thumb, feed your pooch about a ½ teaspoon of coconut oil per 10 pounds of body weight. Since I have little guys, I usually break these bones in half and let them split one. But, depending on what size mold you use and how large your dogs are, that process will differ for you.

INGREDIENTS:

½ cup coconut oil

1 banana

¼ teaspoon ground ginger

NOTES:

 Store in freezer in an airtight container up to one month.

DIRECTIONS:

1 Measure out ½ cup of coconut oil. Melt either in a double boiler or microwave for quick convenience. Melt until there aren't any clumps left.

2 In a small mixing bowl, mash banana with a fork.

3 Add coconut oil to the mixing bowl and whisk until the two ingredients are thoroughly combined. You will be left with a thin pudding-like mixture.

4 Add ¼ teaspoon of ground ginger to your mixture and stir.

5 Grab a silicone mold and fill each bone (or whatever shape mold you're using) to the top.

6 Freeze for 30 minutes, or until set. Store in freezer until ready to serve.

Decoding Coconut Oil Labels

*H*ave you ever walked down the oil aisle of your grocery store and felt overwhelmed by all of the options? Since a lot of my homemade dog treat recipes call for coconut oil, here are some tips to help you choose the best bottle!

Types of Coconut Oil

Unrefined. This simply means the product is not refined. It's pure, raw, or otherwise known as "virgin." Unrefined coconut oil is made from the fresh coconut meat of the whole coconut. Some quick facts:

- No chemicals used in the process.
- Retains more beneficial nutrients.
- Maintains its coconut flavor and aroma.
- Smoke point up to 350°F.

Refined. This type of coconut oil is made from dried coconut meat called copra. During the drying process, there's a potential for bacteria, fungus, dust, bugs, and other impurities to contaminate the copra, so it's bleached and deodorized. The bleaching process is not done with a household type chemical bleach. Rather, it's a filtering process accomplished using a bleaching clay. Some manufacturers say they refine with steam and no chemicals. Read the label carefully. Some quick facts:

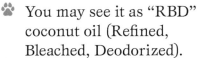

- You may see it as "RBD" coconut oil (Refined, Bleached, Deodorized).
- Some beneficial nutrients are destroyed in the process.
- Neutral coconut smell and taste.

- Smoke point up to 450°F.
- Longer shelf life.
- Cheaper.
- Some low-grade brands are partially hydrogenated.

Processing

Unrefined coconut oil is either cold-pressed or expeller-pressed. With either type, there are no chemicals used in the process. The oils are mechanically squeezed from the coconut meat. The difference in the two types is the temperature used to extract the oil.

- Cold-pressed coconut oil is processed at temperatures up to 120°F.

- Expeller-pressed coconut oil is processed at temperatures up to 210°F.

Refined coconut oil, on the other hand, is processed at temperatures up to 400°F. So you can see why more nutrients are destroyed at this high heat. Most refined coconut oil is bleached and deodorized.

Which Is Healthier?

Unrefined coconut oil has had the least amount of processing. It retains the most nutrients, a natural coconut flavor, and aroma. For its health benefits, unrefined coconut oil is the healthier option.

Organic or Non-Organic?

When it comes to buying coconut oil, always opt for certified organic. It will be labeled USDA Organic. This certifies that the coconuts were grown without the use of pesticides.

Virgin or Extra Virgin?

Of course, when you see coconut oil labeled as "Extra Virgin," it's totally logical to think it has to be better than plain old virgin coconut oil. But is it? Actually, you may be surprised to find out that it's not. It's purely a marketing tease to draw you in and make you think it's the healthier choice. There is actually no "extra virgin" classification for coconut oil. Rather, that classification system is reserved for olive oil. Unrefined coconut oil is virgin and the term "extra virgin" is just a gimmick.

Let's Talk Liquid Coconut Oil

I get a lot of emails about liquid coconut oil. People ask me if they can use liquid coconut oil in my Proud Dog Mom recipes. The answer is no! All of my recipes call for organic, unrefined, virgin, cold-pressed coconut oil. When in this natural state, coconut oil is solid at 76°F and below, and liquid above 76°F. The only way coconut oil can remain in a constant liquid state is to change its composition by decreasing the saturated fats. The main saturated fatty acid targeted for removal is the lauric acid. Since lauric acid has a high melting point of more than 100°F, it has to be removed in order to produce a liquid end product. The down side is, lauric acid is what gives us the majority of health benefits in the coconut oil to begin with, so the more of it you remove, the more potential health benefits you lose.

PBB Paws

These little paws of creamy goodness are nothing more than a mashed banana and couple spoonfuls of peanut butter mixed together. The result? An addicting treat you're definitely going to want to share with your pooch. When making these PBB Paws, make sure you're working with room-temperature peanut butter. This will make the mixing process way easier for you. If you store your peanut butter in the fridge and don't have time to wait for the temp to drop, you can always pop it in the microwave for about 15 seconds.

INGREDIENTS:

1 banana

2 tablespoons organic peanut butter, room temperature

NOTES:

- These PBB Paws maintain a creamy texture once frozen.
- Store in freezer in an airtight container up to one month.

DIRECTIONS:

1 In a small mixing bowl, mash banana with a fork.

2 Add peanut butter and mix together until thoroughly combined.

3 Spoon mixture into a pastry bag. If you don't have a pastry bag, simply pour your mixture into a Ziploc bag and cut one of the edges off.

4 Pipe mixture into paw shaped silicone mold, or mold of your choice.

5 Freeze for about two hours, or until set. Keep in freezer until ready to serve.

Yogurt & Fruit Bark

Get ready for your dog to bark over this yummy yogurt & fruit bark! Not only is it delicious, but it can help your pooch beat the hot summer heat. Plus, it's packed with antioxidants thanks to the blueberries and strawberries. When shopping for yogurt to include in your bark—*or any of the frozen treats in this chapter that call for yogurt*—opt for plain. Avoid artificial flavors, artificial sweeteners, or any other added ingredients. The only thing that should be listed on the ingredient label is pasteurized milk and a few probiotic strains (AKA good bacteria that benefits your pup's gut flora). Since plain yogurt has a rather tart flavor, I like to sweeten it with a moderate amount of raw honey. A quick note on honey, though: Just like a human baby, puppies should not have honey until their immune systems mature. So, if you have a puppy under 1 year old then leave the honey out.

INGREDIENTS:

1 cup plain Greek yogurt
½ cup blueberries
1 tablespoon honey, optional
4 large strawberries

NOTES:

 This yogurt bark is easy to break once frozen.

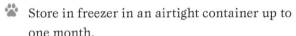 Store in freezer in an airtight container up to one month.

DIRECTIONS:

1. Line a 9x13" baking sheet with parchment paper and set aside.
2. In a blender, mix plain Greek yogurt, blueberries, and honey together.
3. Pour mixture into baking sheet and spread evenly.
4. Slice or chop strawberries and sprinkle on top of mixture.
5. Freeze overnight.
6. In the morning or once set, break yogurt bark into pieces. Sizes will vary depending on the size of your dog.

Pumpkin Patch Frosty Paws

Confession: The first time I made these, the entire pumpkin mixture didn't make it into the molds and freezer. That's right, one little taste turned into two big spoonfuls. They're just too darn delicious. If you're wondering what the dogs thought of them, they agreed! Along with serving these little frosty paws straight up on a hot summer day, they're fun to incorporate into your dog's food bowls. If you already feed your pooch a fresh food diet then you can easily work these healthy pumpkin-based morsels into their homemade meals. If you fill your dog's bowl with kibble, all you have to do is place one on top of their food to melt and enjoy.

INGREDIENTS:

1 cup 100% pure pumpkin purée
1 large carrot, peeled and grated
1 large apple, peeled and grated
1 teaspoon ground chia seeds

NOTES:

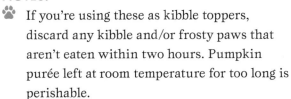 If you're using these as kibble toppers, discard any kibble and/or frosty paws that aren't eaten within two hours. Pumpkin purée left at room temperature for too long is perishable.

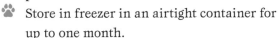 Store in freezer in an airtight container for up to one month.

DIRECTIONS:

1   Put all ingredients into a food processor and blend.
2   Fill silicone molds (or mini muffin tins) with the pumpkin mixture.
3   Freeze overnight. Keep in freezer until ready to serve.

Melt My Heart

This recipe is a fun one to play around with because it's simply puréed fruit mixed with a spoonful of coconut oil. So get creative and play around with dog-friendly fruits such as blueberries, pineapple, mangoes, or watermelon. For this book, I put the spotlight on nutrient-dense strawberries. This beautiful and popular sweet fruit is filled with powerful antioxidants and immune-boosting vitamin C! While strawberries are incredibly healthy for both you and your pooch, they consistently make the Dirty Dozen list—meaning they're ranked one of the most pesticide-laden fruits and veggies on the market. For that reason, I always opt for organic.

INGREDIENTS:

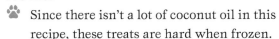
6 large strawberries, washed and tops removed
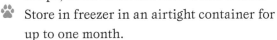
1 tablespoon coconut oil

NOTES:

🐾 Since there isn't a lot of coconut oil in this recipe, these treats are hard when frozen.

🐾 Store in freezer in an airtight container for up to one month.

DIRECTIONS:

1   In a blender, mix strawberries and coconut oil.
2   Pour mixture into silicone heart mold, or another mold of your choice.
3   Freeze for 1 hour, or until set.
4   Keep in freezer until ready to serve.

Fresh Breath Frozen Bites

If you loved the Fresh Breath Biscuits on page 37 then you need to try this frozen recipe too! Made with smell-good herbs, it's pretty much a refreshing frosty breath mint for your dog. While I like to finely chop my mint and parsley leaves first and then mix them into the yogurt with a spoon, if you have a food processor and would prefer to purée the mixture then go for it. It's all about what texture you prefer and what kitchen tools you have on hand. Either way, the prep for these Fresh Breath Frozen Bites is just minutes.

INGREDIENTS:

1 cup plain Greek yogurt

2 sprigs mint leaves, stems removed

2 sprigs parsley leaves, stems removed

1 tablespoon raw honey

NOTES:

- Avoid raw honey if you have a puppy under 1-year-old or a dog with a compromised immune system. That's because raw honey may contain botulism spores. Additionally, avoid honey if your dog is diabetic.
- If you want to make this recipe for your young puppy then simply swap the honey for equal parts organic maple syrup
- Store in freezer in an airtight container for up to one month.

DIRECTIONS:

1 Put Greek yogurt in a mixing bowl and set aside.

2 Finely chop mint and parsley leaves. Add them to the Greek yogurt.

3 Add honey and mix thoroughly.

4 Fill silicone molds with mixture and freeze overnight. Keep in freezer until ready to serve.

Carrot Blueberry Cold Bites

I created this simple treat one afternoon when I had two good dogs waiting by my feet and no biscuits in sight to reward them with. I opened up my refrigerator door and skimmed what was left—I was one day away from a big grocery shop and running low on food. With a few large carrot sticks and a box of fresh blueberries that needed to be eaten, a lightbulb went off. All I needed to do was shred my carrots, mash my blueberries, and mix them with a little coconut oil. Since coconut oil solidifies fast in the freezer, I knew it would be just a matter of minutes until my little loves would get to lick a sweet treat.

INGREDIENTS:
½ cup coconut oil
¼ cup blueberries
1 carrot stick

NOTES:
- In a pinch for time? Rather than mashing the blueberries and grating the carrots, simply throw all the ingredients into a blender and purée.
- The coconut oil doesn't freeze hard like an ice cube so these will be easy for your dog to chew.
- Store in freezer in an airtight container up to one month.

DIRECTIONS:
1. Measure and then melt coconut oil either in a double boiler or the microwave. Set aside.
2. In a small mixing bowl, mash blueberries with a fork. You will be left with small blueberry chunks.
3. Peel and grate carrot.
4. Mix all ingredients in a mixing bowl until thoroughly combined. It may feel like too much carrot, but that's okay.
5. Fill a silicone mold with your mixture.
6. Freeze for 30 minutes, or until set.

Pupcakes

The Recipes

Mushy Middle Muffin Pupcakes

Every day with your dog should be a celebration, but some occasions call for a little extra-special something. So, if you're throwing your dog a birthday party, hosting a holiday dinner, or just want your pooch to feel special then whip up a batch of pupcakes. They're just like cupcakes, but for dogs!

These particular pupcakes are gluten-free, offer a sweet fruity flavor, and are mushy in the middle. You know what that means, right? They're easy for any dog to chew—from puppies who don't have all of their teeth yet to seniors with dental issues. Enjoy!

INGREDIENTS:

1 cup quick oats

½ cup coconut flour

1 medium banana, mashed

½ cup all-natural applesauce

⅔ cup water

3 tablespoons coconut oil (Plus, extra to grease mini muffin tin)

NOTES:

- If your dog is a natural gobbler—one who doesn't really chew before swallowing—you will want to break your pupcake into smaller pieces before serving!

- Store in airtight container in the refrigerator up to two weeks or in the freezer up to three months.

DIRECTIONS:

1. Preheat oven to 350°F.
2. Grease a mini muffin tin with coconut oil and set aside.
3. In a large mixing bowl, add quick oats and coconut flour. Whisk together.
4. In a separate bowl, mix together mashed banana, applesauce, water, and coconut oil.
5. Add wet ingredients to dry ingredients and mix with a spoon until thoroughly combined.
6. Spoon dough into mini muffin tins, filling ¾ full. They will not rise.
7. Bake for 30 minutes.
8. Turn oven off, crack the door open, and let pupcakes cool right inside for about 30 minutes. Check them occasionally to make sure the edges do not burn.

Sandstone Muffins

Buckwheat flour never ceases to amaze me. It's easy to work with, bakes well, and looks awesome! I call these special-occasion treats Sandstone Muffins because looking at their dark, grainy appearance reminds me of a majestic rock. While they may look like they would have a coarser texture, they're actually as soft and smooth as a decadent piece of cake.

INGREDIENTS:

1 cup buckwheat flour
1 tablespoon ground flaxseeds
½ cup applesauce
½ cup water
1 large egg
1 tablespoon coconut oil (Plus, extra to grease mini muffin tin)

NOTES:

- If your dog is a natural gobbler—one who doesn't really chew before swallowing—you will want to break your pupcake into smaller pieces before serving!
- Store in airtight container in the refrigerator up to two weeks or in the freezer up to three months.

DIRECTIONS:

1   Preheat oven to 350°F.
2   Grease a mini muffin tin with coconut oil and set aside.
3   In a mixing bowl, add buckwheat flour and ground flaxseeds. Whisk together and set aside.
4   In a separate bowl, whisk together applesauce, water, egg, and coconut oil.
5   Add wet ingredients to dry ingredients and whisk together until thoroughly combined.
6   Spoon batter/dough into mini muffin tins, filling ¾ full. They will not rise.
7   Bake for 20 minutes. Edges will turn slightly golden brown.
8   Transfer to a wire rack to cool.

Carob Chip Muffins

Okay … so you may have done a double take when you first saw the photo of these pupcakes because they look a whole lot like chocolate chip muffins. In fact, they kind of taste a little like chocolate chip muffins too. But, there's no need to worry because those little chocolate-looking chips are actually carob chips, and they're totally safe for our canine companions.

While chocolate comes from cocoa beans, carob chips are made from the pod of a carob tree. Inside the pod is sweet pulp that is dried, roasted, and ground into a powder. You'll find both carob powder and carob chips in the store. Not only is carob free of the toxic compounds found in chocolate, it also touts a moderate amount of fiber, potassium, and vitamins.

INGREDIENTS:

1½ cups brown rice flour

¼ cup carob chips

½ cup water

1 large egg

2 tablespoons extra virgin olive oil (Plus, extra to grease mini muffin tin)

NOTES:

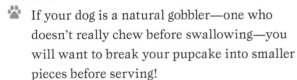 If your dog is a natural gobbler—one who doesn't really chew before swallowing—you will want to break your pupcake into smaller pieces before serving!

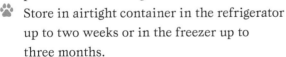 Store in airtight container in the refrigerator up to two weeks or in the freezer up to three months.

DIRECTIONS:

1   Preheat oven to 350°F.

2   Grease a muffin tin with olive oil and set aside.

3   In a mixing bowl, add brown rice flour and carob chips. Whisk together and set aside.

4   In a separate bowl, whisk together water, egg, and olive oil.

5   Add wet ingredients to dry ingredients and mix together with a spoon until you're left with a thick batter.

6   Pour batter into muffin tins, filling ¾ full. They will not rise.

7   Bake for 25 minutes, or until the edges become golden brown.

8   Transfer to a wire rack to cool.

Peanut Butter Pupcakes

The first time I made these pupcakes was for my little Diego's third birthday. Yes, I'm one of those people who throws birthday parties for her dog—although, I usually keep the celebrations pretty low-key with just a few family dogs. Okay, back to the pupcakes. They were a hit among Diego and his party guests. So much so that I decided to share the recipe on my Proud Dog Mom blog. Before I knew it, I was getting messages from other dog parents saying they whipped up a batch for their canine kid's birthday too. While it certainly doesn't have to be your dog's big day to make these, they are a rather special treat. Because, after all, peanut butter!

INGREDIENTS:

1 cup brown rice flour

½ cup coconut flour

½ cup organic peanut butter

½ cup water

1 large egg

2 tablespoons coconut oil (Plus, extra to grease mini muffin tin)

NOTES:

- The texture of this cupcake is more along the lines of a crunchy biscuit versus a fluffy cake.
- If your dog is a natural gobbler—one who doesn't really chew before swallowing—you will want to break your pupcake into smaller pieces before serving!
- Peanut butter frosting shown in photo on page 158.
- Store un-iced pupcakes in airtight container in the refrigerator up to two weeks or in the freezer up to three months.

DIRECTIONS:

1. Preheat oven to 350°F.
2. Grease a muffin tin with coconut oil and set aside.
3. In a large mixing bowl, add brown rice and coconut flours. Whisk together. Set aside.
4. In a separate bowl, mix together peanut butter, water, egg, and coconut oil.
5. Add wet ingredients to dry ingredients and mix together with a spoon or fork until thoroughly combined.
6. If needed, knead dough with your hands until thoroughly combined.
7. Pack dough into mini muffin tins, filling ¾ full. They will not rise.
8. Bake for 18–20 minutes, or until the edges become golden brown.
9. Transfer to a wire rack to cool.

Carrot Spice Cakes

I named these gluten-free pupcakes "Carrot Spice Cakes" because they taste exactly like a pumpkin spice cake. Just to clarify, I'm talking about the popular *human* dessert that seems to take over kitchens across America come the fall. While there isn't actually any pumpkin in this recipe, the light texture and hint of cinnamon make this treat reminiscent of the popular cake. If you're caring for a senior dog with dental issues and looking for an easy treat for him/her to chew, this would be perfect since the inside is incredibly soft and doesn't require a lot of chewing.

INGREDIENTS:

Coconut oil, to grease mini muffin tin
1 cup brown rice flour
½ teaspoon cinnamon
1 cup finely grated carrots
2 large eggs
½ cup water
2 tablespoons honey

NOTES:

- Avoid raw honey if you have a puppy under 1-year-old or a dog with a compromised immune system. That's because raw honey may contain botulism spores. Additionally, avoid honey if your dog is diabetic.
- If your dog is a natural gobbler—one who doesn't really chew before swallowing—you will want to break your pupcake into smaller pieces before serving!
- Store in airtight container in the refrigerator for up to one-two weeks or in the freezer up to three months.

DIRECTIONS:

1. Preheat oven to 350°F.
2. Grease a muffin tin with coconut oil and set aside.
3. In a large mixing bowl, add brown rice flour and cinnamon. Whisk together. Set aside.
4. In a separate bowl, mix together grated carrots, eggs, water, and honey.
5. Add wet ingredients to dry ingredients and mix together with a spoon until thoroughly combined.
6. Spoon batter into muffin tins, filling ¾ full. They will not rise.
7. Bake for 20 minutes, or until the edges become golden brown.
8. Transfer to a wire rack to cool.

Go Gourmet: All-Natural Icings

The Recipes

All-Natural Icings

Have you ever seen gourmet treats from a doggy bakery? They're usually topped with brightly colored icings and feature fun, funky patterns. Some are blue and pink, others are green and orange. Some have polka dots, others have stripes. No matter how they're decorated, though, they're all really cute! Sure, adding icing to your homemade treats won't make your dog's tail wag any harder, but the sight of a pretty bone will certainly make you and your dog-loving friends smile. I don't personally ice my homemade dog treats on a regular basis, but I do love to add the special accent for occasions—holidays, parties, birthdays, and gifts. The next few pages of this book are filled with icing recipes. You'll notice a few patterns among these recipes. For starters, they almost all use plain Greek yogurt for the base.

Like I mentioned in the Pupsicles chapter, make sure your yogurt doesn't have any artificial flavors or sweeteners. Secondly, I've added a small amount of tapioca flour to almost every icing recipe—this helps to create a thicker icing. So, if you're trying to add little designs and find a particular icing is still too thin then you can always just add a little more tapioca flour to the mix. Lastly, you will notice that I don't use any artificial food coloring to make my colorful icings. Since I like to stay as natural as possible, I use healthy fruit purées and other dog approved ingredients to create colors. Need a color that I haven't included? I hope the recipes in this chapter spark your inner creative Dog Chef and inspire you to play around in the kitchen!

NOTES:

- Most of the icing recipes in the chapter will stiffen when dry.
- Ice treats the day you plan to serve them.
- Store iced treats in an airtight container in the refrigerator or freezer. Storage will vary depending on the treat.

- Avoid raw honey if you have a puppy under 1-year-old or a dog with a compromised immune system. That's because raw honey may contain botulism spores. Additionally, avoid honey if your dog is diabetic.
- Store iced treats in an airtight container in the refrigerator or freezer. Storage will vary depending on the treat.

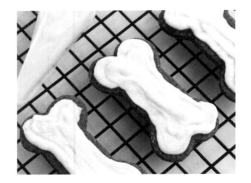

White Yogurt Icing

INGREDIENTS:

¼ cup plain Greek yogurt

3 tablespoons tapioca flour

1 tablespoon honey

DIRECTIONS:

1   In a small mixing bowl, whisk all ingredients together.

2   Frost your treats!

Pink Yogurt Icing

INGREDIENTS:

¼ cup plain Greek yogurt

3 fresh medium-sized strawberries

¼ cup tapioca flour

1 tablespoon honey

DIRECTIONS:

1   Use a high-speed blender to thoroughly combine all ingredients.

2   Frost your treats!

Blue Yogurt Icing

INGREDIENTS:

¼ cup plain Greek yogurt

¼ cup fresh blueberries

¼ cup tapioca flour

1 tablespoon honey

DIRECTIONS:

1   Use a high-speed blender to thoroughly combine all ingredients.

2   Frost your treats!

Peanut Butter Icing

INGREDIENTS:

¼ cup plain Greek yogurt

2 tablespoons organic peanut butter

DIRECTIONS:

1   In a small bowl, mix ingredients together.

2   Frost your treats!

Pumpkin Icing

INGREDIENTS:

¼ cup plain Greek yogurt

3 tablespoons tapioca flour

2 tablespoons 100% pure pumpkin purée

1 tablespoon honey

DIRECTIONS:

1 In a small mixing bowl, whisk ingredients together.

2 Frost your treats!

Carob Icing

INGREDIENTS:

Water

½ cup carob chips

1 tablespoon coconut oil

DIRECTIONS:

1 Fill a saucepan ⅓ way full with water and bring to a boil.

2 Once water reaches a rolling boil, turn it down to a simmer.

3 Place a heatproof bowl on top of saucepan. It should fit tightly on top of the saucepan and shouldn't touch the water. Make sure no steam gets into the bowl—it will ruin your melt.

4 Put carob chips and coconut oil into the bowl. After a couple of minutes start to mix them around. Continue mixing until mixture reaches a smooth consistency and has no more lumps.

5 Ice biscuits.

NOTES:

🐾 Melting carob can be a little tricky. It doesn't melt as easily as chocolate. Some people choose to melt it in the microwave, but quite honestly, it's never worked well for me. I find the easiest way to melt carob chips is in a double boiler on the stovetop.

🐾 Do not make this icing ahead of time. Make it when you are ready to use it because you can't successfully melt carob a second time.

Cracking the Carob Code

*O*ne of the things you learn as a new puppy parent is what human foods are safe for your pooch to eat and which ones are major no-nos. Chocolate definitely tops the no list—*theobromine and caffeine are two compounds in chocolate that stimulate the nervous system, which can cause severe symptoms.* While most of us know that chocolate is toxic to canines, have you ever noticed a chocolate-looking coating on gourmet dog biscuits? What's that about? Well, there's no need to worry because that coating isn't chocolate. It's carob … which is super tasty and totally safe for your dog.

What Is Carob?

Origin. While chocolate comes from cocoa beans, carob chips are made from the pod of a carob tree. Inside the pod is sweet pulp that is dried, roasted, and ground into a powder. You'll find both carob powder and carob chips in the store.

Taste. Carob is naturally sweet and tends to have a nuttier flavor than chocolate.

Nutritional Content. Not only is carob free of the toxic compounds found in chocolate, it also touts a moderate amount of fiber, potassium, and vitamins.

How I Use Carob

I like to use carob as a way to jazz up special occasion treats—either by sprinkling a few carob chips into my dough to make carob-chip pupcakes (like on page 149) or by melting the chips in a double boiler to create a biscuit icing (like on page 159).

Holiday Celebration
Treats

The Recipes

Americana

Whether you're honoring the fallen troops on Memorial Day, hosting a July 4th picnic, or saying goodbye to summer vacation with a Labor Day party, why not toss your pooch a patriotic treat? Nicknamed the Americana, these red, white, and blue stars are made with antioxidant-rich blueberries and strawberries. You can use either coconut oil or yogurt for the base *(the stars featured in the photo on the last page are made with coconut oil).* As you skim down the ingredient list, you will notice that I haven't included quantities. That's because everyone is going to use a different size mold and will need a different amount. So, adjust as necessary!

INGREDIENTS:
Coconut oil *or* plain Greek yogurt
Blueberries
Strawberries, diced

NOTES:
 Store in freezer until ready to serve.
 Store in freezer in an airtight container up to one month.

DIRECTIONS:
1   If using coconut oil as your base, melt down to a liquid state either in a double boiler or the microwave.
2   Fill a star-shaped silicone mold ¼ way up with either coconut oil *or* plain yogurt.
3   Add one blueberry and one slice of strawberry in each star (more if you're using a large mold).
4   Top each star off with coconut oil *or* plain yogurt, filling each to the top.
5   Freeze until set—coconut oil freezes quicker than yogurt.

Doggy Deviled Eggs

Nothing says Easter quite like eggs, don't you agree? This Easter, let your dog join in on the holiday celebration by making these doggie deviled eggs. I've transformed this popular dish into a totally dog-friendly treat by swapping out the fatty mayo for plain Greek yogurt and adding some tail-wagging good salmon to the mix. This easy-to-make recipe will leave you with half a dozen Doggy Deviled Eggs.

INGREDIENTS:

3 hard-boiled eggs
½ can wild caught salmon, in water (approximately 2½ oz)
2 tablespoons plain Greek yogurt

NOTES:

 Store in airtight container in the refrigerator up to three days.

DIRECTIONS:

1   Cut hard-boiled eggs in half, remove yolks, and put yolks in a small mixing bowl.
2   With a fork, finely mash egg yolks. Set aside.
3   Open and drain canned salmon. Drain until dry!
4   Add drained salmon and yogurt to mashed egg yolks and thoroughly combine.
5   Spoon or pipe egg mixture into the center of each egg, creating 6 doggy deviled eggs.

Spooktacular Howl-O-Ween Biscuits

Halloween is a holiday filled with spooky decor, fun costumes, and a whole lot of candy. While your pooch can't indulge in the same sweet treats as we can, he still deserves a little something special. Enter these gluten-free peanut butter pumpkin biscuits shaped into mummies, pumpkins, bats, witch hats, broom sticks, and skulls. There are a bunch of different Halloween cookie cutters—use whichever you have! Along with making these biscuits for my two pups, I usually bake a big batch every October and then stuff them into little holiday themed treat bags. They get my canine trick-or-treat visitors pretty excited!

INGREDIENTS:

2 cups oat flour

1 cup almond flour

1 cup 100% pure pumpkin purée

½ cup organic peanut butter

1 egg

NOTES:

- Frosting recipe on page 158.
- Use room temperature peanut butter for easy mixing.
- Store un-iced treats in airtight container in the refrigerator up to two weeks or in the freezer up to three months.

DIRECTIONS:

1 Preheat oven to 350°F.

2 Line two baking sheets with parchment paper and set aside.

3 Add oat and almond flour to a large mixing bowl and whisk together. Set aside.

4 In a separate bowl, mix pumpkin, peanut butter, and egg until thoroughly combined.

5 Add wet ingredients to dry ingredients and mix together with a fork or spoon.

6 With your hands, knead dough for several minutes, eventually forming a dough ball.

7 Let dough rest on the counter for 5 minutes.

8 Sandwich dough ball between two sheets of parchment paper and roll flat (about ¼" thick) with a rolling pin.

9 Using a cookie cutter, stamp out biscuits.

10 Place biscuits on baking sheet.

11 Bake for 25–30 minutes, depending on how thick your biscuits are.

12 Transfer biscuits to a wire rack to cool.

Sweet Potato Pup Fries

When I was a little girl I remember thinking that sweet potatoes only existed to cushion marshmallows on Thanksgiving. In my mind, that was their purpose. Does your family make a sweet potato marshmallow casserole on Thanksgiving, too? Well, as I've matured, I've come to realize sweet potatoes don't only taste amazing, but they're a healthy treat for both us humans and our canines. So your pooch feels included in your Thanksgiving feast, make some of these sweet potato pup fries. They're pretty much the same as human sweet potato fries, but I haven't loaded them with any extra spices. They're simply baked sweet potato coated in a little bit of olive oil. I think your dog will definitely give thanks for these fries.

INGREDIENTS:
1 large sweet potato
1 tablespoon extra-virgin olive oil

NOTES:
Store in airtight container in the refrigerator up to three days.

DIRECTIONS:
1   Preheat oven to 425°F.
2   Line one or two baking sheets with parchment paper and set aside.
3   Using a mandolin or knife, slice sweet potato into sticks/fries (about ¼"–½" thick).
4   Put sweet potato strips in a mixing bowl and coat with olive oil.
5   With your hands, massage the oil evenly into the sweet potato sticks.
6   Place coated sweet potatoes on a baking sheet—not touching.
7   Bake for 15 minutes.
8   Flip fries over and bake for another 10 minutes.
9   Remove from oven and let cool on baking sheet.

Pumpkin Pie Paws

I think the best part of a Thanksgiving feast is dessert. Who's with me? One popular holiday dish that earns a spot on many people's table is pumpkin pie. *Oh, I'm drooling just thinking about it!* While traditional pumpkin pie is loaded with spices that aren't good for our canine kids, that doesn't mean they can't indulge in a healthy dog-approved version. That's where this flourless pumpkin pie shaped into a paw print comes in. This delicate treat is very moist and creamy—a texture reminiscent to the real thing. Plus, with only four ingredients that just need to be dumped into a mixing bowl and stirred together, this recipe won't add a lot of extra work to your holiday prep to-do list.

INGREDIENTS:

½ cup 100% pure pumpkin purée

1 egg

1 tablespoon honey *or* 100% pure maple syrup

½ teaspoon cinnamon

NOTES:

 Avoid raw honey if you have a puppy under 1-year-old or a dog with a compromised immune system. That's because raw honey may contain botulism spores. Additionally, avoid honey if your dog is diabetic.

 Store in airtight container in the refrigerator up to three days.

DIRECTIONS:

1   Preheat oven to 350°F.

2   In a mixing bowl, thoroughly combine all ingredients.

3   Spoon mixture into a silicone mold.

4   Bake for 30 minutes.

5   Remove from oven and let cool in mold.

Need a Gift? Give Dog Treats

When it comes to gift giving, people always get a kick out of receiving a homemade present. There's just something special about knowing a person invested the time and energy to make a custom creation with the hopes of putting a smile on your face. If you're in search of a thoughtful, cute, and affordable gift for a fellow dog lover in your life, then whipping up a batch of dog treats is a great idea! Not only are people excited that you thought of their four-legged children, but you can wrap the treats in a cute mug or beautiful canister that they'll be able to hold onto forever.

Beautifully wrapped dog treats are perfect for a variety of occasions—bring them along to a house party to thank the host, create a care package for new dog parents, or give them as a casual Christmas/birthday gift. They also make great party favors if you're hosting a celebration where both humans and canines attend.

When gifting dog treats, get crafty and have some fun. Here are some cute ideas to get you started:

🐾 Try packing them in a pastry box for your friend who appreciates good bakery. You can usually find a set of cheap yet high-quality pastry boxes at your local craft store.

🐾 Stuff them in a mason jar for that co-worker who always brings overnight oats or salad jars to the office.

🐾 Fill a pastry bag with dog treats and stuff them in a cute coffee mug for the coffee lover in your life.

🐾 Buy a fancy new dog bowl, fill it with dog treats, and wrap it with shrink wrap for your friend who just adopted a new pooch.

🐾 Hosting a dog-friendly movie night? Stuff treats in a popcorn bag and design the outside with doggie stickers.

Enjoy!

Christmas Cookies

Remember The Basic Biscuit back on page 33? Well, it's here again! Only this time, I've added sliced strawberries and chopped mint leaves into the mix.

Not only is the strawberry/mint combo a yummy one that will get your dog's tail wagging, the pops of red and green are perfect for Christmas. *Ho, Ho, Ho!*

INGREDIENTS:

3 cups oat flour
1 cup coconut flour
3 fresh strawberries
¼ cup fresh mint leaves
2 large eggs
1 cup water
¼ cup coconut oil

NOTES:

 Are the center of your biscuits softer than you'd like? Instead of removing them from the oven, simply turn the oven off, crack the door open, and let the biscuits cool right inside. They will continue to dry out in the gradually fading heat. *Watch carefully to ensure they don't burn.*

Store in airtight container in the refrigerator up to one week or in the freezer up to three months.

DIRECTIONS:

1   Preheat oven to 350°F.
2   Line two baking sheets with parchment paper. Set aside.
3   Add oat and coconut flours to a mixing bowl. Whisk together until thoroughly combined. Set aside.
4   Slice fresh strawberries and finely chop mint leaves—just the leaves, avoid the stems. Add to flours and whisk together.
5   Make a well in the center of the dry ingredients and add remaining wet ingredients. Mix together with a spoon or fork.
6   With your hands, knead dough for several minutes, eventually forming a dough ball.
7   Sandwich dough ball between two sheets of parchment paper and roll flat (about ¼" thick) with a rolling pin.
8   Using a cookie cutter, stamp out biscuits.
9   Place biscuits on a parchment paper-lined baking sheet and bake for 25–30 minutes.
10 Transfer biscuits to a wire rack to cool.

Acknowledgements

When my mom and I decided to partner up and start our blog on January 1, 2016, we had no clue how many amazing people it would connect us with. From veterinarians and trainers to dog-focused app developers and fellow pet bloggers, we feel extremely grateful to have met every single one of you. We truly value the people who stand up and act as a positive voice for the canine community. It's really heartwarming to see how many people out there are working together to spread the word about the health and well-being of our furry best friends. Your support and well wishes really mean the world to us.

To Modi Ramos and the rest of the iHeartDogs.com team, thank you for all of your support. It's been an amazing experience to host a mini cooking segment for your Facebook following, and I value your continued support with this cookbook.

Since launching Proud Dog Mom, we've had an overwhelming response from readers—whom I've nicknamed the Proud Dog Mom Pack! We love waking up to your emails every morning and hearing about your dog parenting experiences. We find a lot of inspiration through your questions, comments, and suggestions. Just know, we read everything that you send, and we try our best to provide the tools you need to raise your pooch. If it wasn't for your genuine interest in learning to cook for your dog(s), this book wouldn't exist.

To Sam, my dear friend, talented photographer, photo editor, and founder of Peaberry Photography, I thank you for taking the amazing lifestyle photos that appear throughout this book. I also want to say a big thank you for the many hours you spent on the phone with me, guiding me as I snapped and edited each food photo. You really understood my vision and were a huge inspiration for which photos ultimately made it into this book.

Of course, I have to say a huge thanks to my two dogs—Diego and Gigi—and my mom's dogs—Tina and Pippa. They are our ultimate inspiration and our main taste testers. I know tasting all of the treats in this book—from the biscuits to the jerky strips—is a hard job, but someone had to do it. Sure, they got a little help from other dogs around my community (plus, the many dogs around the world who enjoy the recipes on our blog). But Diego, Gigi, Tina, and Pippa certainly rose to the occasion. They woke up extra early and stayed up super late just to sit by our feet and wait for the next tray of treats to come out of the oven.

Meet the Authors

Mother/daughter duo Donna and Melissa are the founders, recipe creators, photographers, editors, video creators, and writers behind the hit blog ProudDogMom.com— the ultimate spot for everything canine. The two have raised pooches for decades and work closely with groomers, trainers, veterinarians, dog product developers, and more. Despite living on two different sides of the country, Melissa and Donna had a mission to come together and share their knowledge and resources with other proud dog moms around the world. You can find their blog online at ProudDogMom.com.